SMART BREAKFASTS

101 Delicious, Healthy Ways to Start the Day

JANE KINDERLEHRER

Illustrations by Carol Inouye

NEWMARKET PRESS

New York

Dedicated to
my beloved breakfast companion
who lights up my mornings and my life

Copyright © 1989 by Jane Kinderlehrer

This book published simultaneously
in the United States of America and in Canada.

Library of Congress Cataloging-in-Publication Data
Kinderlehrer, Jane.
  Smart breakfasts.

  Includes index.
  1. Breakfasts. I. Title.
TX733.K56 1989   641.5′2   89-12610
ISBN 1-55704-045-1

BOMC offers recordings and compact discs, cassettes
and records. For information and catalog write to
BOMR, Camp Hill, PA 17012.

Book design by Ruth Kolbert
Manufactured in the United States

Contents

METRIC CONVERSION CHART

1 teaspoon = 5 ml.   1 tablespoon = 15 ml.

1 ounce = 30 ml.   1 cup = 240 ml./.24 l.

1 quart = 950 ml./.95 l.   1 gallon = 3.80 l.

1 ounce = 28 gr.   1 pound = 454 gr./.454 kg.

F°	200	225	250	275	300	325	350	375	400	425	450
C°	93	107	121	135	149	163	177	191	204	218	232

ABBREVIATIONS

cal = calories   sat = saturated

pro = protein   unsat = unsaturated

g = gram

INTRODUCTION

Wake Up Your Life
with Smart Breakfasts

"Eat breakfast like a king, lunch like a prince, and dinner like a pauper." This time-honored advice to those in search of good health is still very good counsel and can enhance your chances both of living it up and living longer. Researchers at the University of California found that longevity rates were 60 percent higher for men and 72 percent higher for women who ate breakfast "almost every day" compared to those who "rarely ate breakfast."

And, just as important for today's health-conscious person, you can indulge in a royal breakfast without gaining unwanted pounds and without compromising your coronary arteries.

How? By eating a Smart Breakfast! The world will become your kingdom. You will feel a wonderful sense of well-being that flows through your veins like champagne bubbles. You will look better and perform better.

Isn't it wonderful that something as enjoyable as eating breakfast every day can contribute so much zest to living, while it strengthens your lease on life?

WHAT IS A SMART BREAKFAST?

It's not doughnuts or Danishes and coffee or an empty-calorie, sugar-coated cereal. These rapidly absorbed carbos boost the blood sugar, causing a rush of insulin, which then removes all the sugar from your blood. This, in turn, deprives your brain of glucose, without which you can't think straight. Come mid-morning, you feel desperately hungry. Your willpower bottoms out and you reach for a doughnut, croissant, or candy bar.

But it doesn't have to be that way. A Smart Breakfast is a meal which provides at least 15 grams of protein for stamina and mental alertness; nutrient-dense carbohydrates for sustained energy; about

10 grams of fat for stick-to-your-ribs satiety and for the essential fatty acids that strengthen your immune system; and fruit or juice for vitamin C, to enhance absorption of iron, calcium, and other minerals. It provides about 500 calories, is low in sodium and rich in fibers (about 10 grams), to promote colon health and lower cholesterol levels. And its great flavor and texture brings pleasure to your taste buds.

NO MORE EXCUSES!

The beauty of a smart breakfast is that it makes it so hard for anyone to hang on to bad habits. All those well-worn reasons why you can get by without a smart breakfast pale against the reasons why you really can't.

Eat a Good Breakfast to Lose Weight

One of the most frequent excuses I hear for skipping breakfast is, "I'm on a diet."

If you are skipping breakfast in order to lose weight, STOP! You are defeating your purpose. You are keeping the motors of your metabolic machinery in low gear. What you want to do, in order to burn fat, is shift into high. Your body will burn your breakfast calories much more easily than the calories you consume at dinner.

When you skip breakfast, you suffer mid-morning slump and hunger, making you more vulnerable to weight-producing snack attacks. To lose weight and feel great, do exactly the opposite of saving calories: Invest them wisely in a smart breakfast.

To Save Time, Eat Breakfast

Maybe you think you have no time for breakfast. Think again. A Smart Breakfast can so enhance your efficiency you will actually save time. I know that mornings can be hectic and a rush for survival. But with a little planning the night before, and with the help of time-saving appliances like the microwave oven, breakfast can be ready in less time than it takes to brush your teeth.

On those mornings when you have no time to eat, use your blender or food processor and *drink* your breakfast.

No time to eat or drink? Take a portable breakfast along. Eat it at the bus stop, at red lights, or in traffic snafus. You'll be grateful for delays instead of cursing them. Take-along breakfasts will also quash those mid-morning hunger pangs that lead to unwise snack attacks. (See the chapter on "Smart Breakfasts in a Hurry.")

Wake Up with a Hearty Appetite

"But I'm just not hungry in the morning!"

If the thought of eating breakfast just turns you off, you probably ate your breakfast calories the night before. You rationalized that you deserved that piece of pie, ice-cream sundae, or bag of chips—because you'll skip breakfast in the morning. This is not smart thinking. Nighttime snacking not only kills your appetite for breakfast, it contributes to weight gain and deficiencies in the important nutrients you should be getting at breakfast.

To break the cycle, try a late-afternoon snack—a few nuts or sunflower seeds, a cup of popcorn, raw carrots, or sprouted garbanzo beans—to take the edge off your appetite for the evening meal. And go to bed early, before you get snack-happy. You'll wake up ravenous!

If you still don't wake up hungry, it's perfectly all right to delay breakfast for an hour or so after rising. Have a piece of fruit, then take a morning walk or a jog around the block to perk up your appetite. Or, if you must leave for school or work, bag breakfast and take it with you.

Can't Have Wheat or Dairy?
Try Smart Breakfasts for the Allergic

If you are one of the 50 million people in this country who suffer from food allergies, see the chapter on "Smart Breakfasts for the Allergic." There are many wonderful smart breakfasts that eliminate the most common food allergens. For instance, if you can't handle wheat, you can learn how to cook millet, buckwheat, rice, and beans in many tantalizing dishes.

Smart Kids Eat Smart Breakfasts

"I wish I could get my children to eat something other than those sugary cereals." This is the most common complaint I hear at the lectures I give. It is, indeed, a matter of concern. Consider that researchers are finding a definite link between junk-food diets and abnormal behavior. "Excessive sugar is definitely related to deviant behavior," says criminologist Alexander Schauss in his book *Diet, Crime, and Delinquency*. Sugar and refined carbohydrates use up the body's supplies of thiamine. Blood tests indicate that many juveniles who get into trouble are thiamine-deficient, which causes depression, insomnia, chronic fatigue, and erratic behavior.

What's a parent to do when the foods that contribute to health are considered "yukky"? Nagging doesn't work, and you can't force kids or feed them intravenously. Hold on to your sense of humor and go creative with the dishes you serve. They may refuse ordinary pancakes, but they'll love "Funny Face Fluffy Pancakes." And try sneaking in the good stuff. What six-year-old Little League hopeful can refuse a tablespoon of "Muscle Power" in his yogurt, and what would-be cheerleader doesn't want a sprinkle of "Complexion Beauty" on her cereal? (Only you need know that it's all wheat germ!) See "Smart Breakfasts for the Small Fry" for other ideas.

And if your children—or you—just don't cotton to breakfast foods, why not eat lunch for breakfast? There's nothing wrong with tuna, chicken, or egg salad on whole wheat toast or pita, or cottage cheese with fresh fruit, or baked potatoes with help-yourself toppings. One of my grandchildren likes pizza for breakfast and another warms up last night's lasagna. Using the microwave, just about anything is ready in less than 5 minutes. (See Chapter 9, "Dinner for Breakfast.")

Teenagers vs. Breakfast

Even though your teenager seems to be forever snacking, studies indicate that teenagers are actually the poorest-fed members of the American family. This is most unfortunate because a poor diet at this time of life sets the stage for later problems, such as heart disease, allergies, excess weight, and emotional disturbances.

Why are teenagers so poorly nourished? On the whole, many surveys reveal, they tend to skip breakfast because they are rushed or trying to achieve a glamorous figure. Then they get snack-happy and tend to pig out on empty-calorie foods.

With all children, from toddlers to teens, it's wise to do as much breakfast preparation as possible the night before. Get them up in plenty of time. Relaxed, they'll begin to feel better about themselves, more alert, more energetic, and more able to cope. Serve them a Smart Breakfast and soon they will insist on it and even prepare it themselves when you oversleep. There is enough variety in these chapters to satisfy their very individual tastes and preferences.

Elegant Celebration Breakfasts

Just because a breakfast is smart doesn't mean it has to be boring. Weekend breakfasts can be elegant, relaxed, leisurely, bountiful, even romantic. Just being all together in a peaceful, unhurried atmosphere surrounded by aromas that warm the spirit is a celebration.

This is the time to indulge your fancy for once-in-a-while foods: bagels with tangy spreads, delicate soufflés, apricot almond coffee cake, ambrosia cream, crepes with luscious fillings, and pecan waffles. (For more ideas, turn to the "Elegant Weekend Breakfasts" chapter.)

START NOW

It has been said that, at the final reckoning, we shall all be called to account for any permitted pleasures we failed to enjoy. Start now to enjoy the pleasure of the marvelous way you're going to feel when you start each day with a Smart Breakfast.

THE FIBER STORY

The standard American diet, with its average fiber intake of 5 to 10 grams a day, is far below the level required for optimal intestinal function. The National Cancer Institute recommends 25 to 30 grams per day.

Fiber has been shown to increase stool bulk and help speed the movement of food through the digestive track, thus helping to prevent constipation and colon cancer. It also protects against gall bladder disease and unfriendly fats, significantly reducing the incidence of cardiovascular disease.

Your daily fiber intake need not come from cereal alone, so don't try to get it all at breakfast. Studies suggesting that fiber reduces the number of cancer cases are based on populations that eat reasonable amounts of fiber *throughout each day*. Whole grains, vegetables, fruits, beans, and nuts are excellent sources of many different kinds of fiber.

You can increase your fiber intake if, instead of just drinking juice, you eat the whole orange, grapefruit, or apple. Wash but don't peel the apple, and you will be getting more pectin, a very important type of fiber which regulates blood sugar, lowers cholesterol, and helps usher toxic substances out of the body. If you can't find unsprayed apples, give them a 15-minute vinegar bath (¼ cup of vinegar in a 2-quart dishpan), then rinse.

Eat the white inner rind of the orange or grapefruit, and you'll get more fiber and more bioflavonoids, essential to the building of collagen, a substance which is said to strengthen your tissues and delay the signs of aging. Eat whole baked potatoes, skin and all. If you are hooked on mashed potatoes, mash them with the peel. Switch to brown rice—it has 3 times as much fiber as unenriched white.

Wheat Bran

Smart breakfasts are high in many kinds of fiber, including wheat bran. Wheat bran is a water-insoluble fiber. It has been shown to speed the passage of food through the intestines and prevent many digestive and colon problems, and has proven to be the most effective fiber to act against intestinal cancer.

Wheat bran also provides potassium, manganese, iron, calcium, the B vitamin niacin, traces of thiamine, riboflavin, and a smidgeon of unsaturated fat. It can be added to cooked and uncooked cereals, soups, baked goods, beverages, and confections. Because bran absorbs a great deal of fluid, increase your consumption of liquids. Start gradually to increase your bran intake; too rapid an increase can cause diarrhea and flatulence. Be sure to keep your wheat bran refrigerated or in the freezer. (It can be used directly from the freezer.)

Oat Bran

Oat bran, which has been enjoying considerable popularity recently as a cholesterol-lowering food, is rich in water-soluble fiber. Unlike the insoluble fiber found in wheat bran, which helps speed food through the intestinal tract, soluble fiber delays transit time through the small intestine, where it absorbs cholesterol before it gets into the bloodstream.

Research indicates that oat bran significantly lowers both cholesterol and LDL, the harmful stuff that contributes to hardening of the arteries. Dr. James Anderson, a pioneer in oat bran research at the University of Kentucky College of Medicine, recommends a minimum of 6 grams and a maximum of 10 grams of soluble fiber per day to lower serum cholesterol. A 1-ounce serving of oat bran (about ⅓ cup) provides about 3 grams of soluble fiber.

Does that mean you have to eat 2 or 3 bowls of oat bran cereal every day? Not at all. There are many tasty ways to use oat bran. Add it to hot and cold cereals, to pancake and waffle batters. Bake it in muffins, cakes, and cookies. It's a wonderful thickening agent for soups. Many recipes in *Smart Breakfasts* call for at least 2 tablespoons of oat bran.

Don't make the mistake of thinking that just because you're eating oat bran you can overindulge in the bad stuff. Oat bran is most effective when consumed in conjunction with a low-fat, low-cholesterol, high-fiber diet.

Rice Bran

Rice bran is the new "kernel" in the army of cholesterol fighters—and may surpass them all in effectiveness. New research conducted by scientists at the U.S. Department of Agriculture reveals that rice bran can lower blood cholesterol levels as well as or better than oat bran.

Rice bran is the outside layer of the rice kernel, the part that is removed from brown rice to make white rice. It is rich in protein and an excellent source of the vitamin Bs, especially thiamine, the "morale vitamin" and an aid to cell growth and development, and niacin, which is another cholesterol fighter. But that's not all. It's also a veritable gold mine of minerals, providing goodly amounts of calcium, iron, copper, magnesium, and zinc. Because it has no gluten, it can be safely consumed by those who are allergic to most grains.

Rice bran has a nutty-brown color. It has a finer texture and sweeter flavor than oat bran. You can add it to hot and cold breakfast cereals, beverages, and baked goods for more fiber and the glow of health.

BACK TO BASICS WITH PROTEIN

The word *protein* is derived from the Greek word *protos*, which means first, denoting that proteins are of first importance.

Protein is the basic raw material of all living tissue, both plant and animal. Your body is about 20 percent protein by weight. Your heart, brain, lungs, eyes, hair, skin, nerves, and blood cells are constantly being repaired and nourished by the 22 amino acids that make up the protein chain. Of these 22 amino acids, 14 are synthesized by the body and are therefore classified as nonessential. There are 8 that are called essential because the body cannot make them. They must be provided by your food and must be present in the right proportions, preferably at the same meal.

The egg provides such a nearly perfect high-quality protein that it is used as a standard by which to evaluate the quality of protein in all other foods. It supplies your body with all the essential amino acids in the proportions needed to manufacture protein. Fish, meat, poultry, and dairy products closely approximate the amino acid formula the body requires.

Other food sources like grains, nuts, seeds, legumes (peas and beans), starchy vegetables, and fruits are wonderful complex carbohydrate foods that are rich in essential vitamins and minerals, and do provide some of the essential amino acids, but not all of them in the required amounts. However, that does not mean that you cannot enjoy complete high-quality protein from these foods. Two sources from different families may each provide what the other lacks. For instance, grains and beans are a good marriage. Five parts of a whole-grain food plus one part legume eaten together provide a high-quality protein just as complete as meat.

There are many ways you can take advantage of complementary proteins. The recipes in this book have been devised to give you the combinations that makes for high-quality proteins.

How much protein do we need? The Dietary Allowance Committee of the National Academy of Sciences estimates the daily need to be 0.8 grams per kilogram of body weight, which amounts to about 1 gram for every 2 pounds of body weight. Pregnant and lactating women need more, and children need proportionately more to provide the raw material for growth.

When your breakfast provides at least ⅓ of your daily protein needs—about 15 to 22 grams—blood sugar remains above fasting level, you have a sense of well-being, you don't feel hungry, and your level of efficiency remains high for the rest of the day. To help you achieve this state of well-being, each recipe in *Smart Breakfasts* gives you a protein count.

WE ALL NEED SOME FAT

Fat—it's not all bad. Fat provides energy, insulates the body against temperature changes, and helps you utilize the fat-soluble vitamins—A, D, E, and K—which function in tandem with other vitamins and minerals. So don't cut fats out of your diet completely, even if you're overweight.

The trouble is, most Americans get too much fat. High-fat diets have been linked to increased levels of cardiovascular disease and cancer of the breast and colon.

Many health professionals feel we would be wise to cut our fat intake to 20 percent of total calories. At present the American Heart Association's Dietary Goals suggest that no more than 30 percent of calories come from fat and that no more than 10 percent of that 30 percent should be *saturated* fat.

It's the saturated fats that lead to increased levels of serum cholesterol. In nature, they are found mostly in dairy products, meat, lard, and other animal products. You can cut down on them by eating fewer meat products, by using dairy products that are chiefly low-fat and, if you love butter, by using Healthy Heart Butter (see index for recipe).

But there are other, less obvious culprits. Margarines, solid shortenings, processed cheeses, hydrogenated peanut butter, and packaged cake mixes, along with many other processed foods, contain saturated fats as well.

Other sources of hidden saturated fats are the tropical oils of coconut, palm, and palm kernel. They are more highly saturated than meat. They are used in many foods—margarines, coffee creamers, dessert toppings, chocolates, cereals, many processed foods, and even infant formulas. When a label says "pure vegetable oil" without specifying which oil, it could be one of these tropical oils. Food manufacturers, now aware of the problem, are in the process of switching. So *read the labels*.

Butter vs. Margarine

Pure sweet butter is better than salted butter, and butter made from certified raw cream is the best of all. You'll find raw milk butter in health food stores. It's expensive but well worth the extra dollar.

The trouble with butter is its saturated fat content. By law, butter must be 80 percent milkfat. As much as 65 percent of that fat is saturated. Healthy Heart Butter has half the saturated-fat content and, instead, is combined with beneficial mono- and polyunsaturated oils. Whenever butter is called for in these recipes, or in any recipe, you will be doing your health and your family's health a big favor if you substitute Healthy Heart Butter. Tastewise, they'll never know the difference.

You can also spread butter thinner on bread, toast, or pancakes. Don't add it to cooked vegetables. Instead, substitute herbs, lemon juice, a little broth, a little olive oil, or tomato sauce.

Do not be tempted to substitute margarine for butter. There is no comparison in taste, and healthwise, you're much better off with butter, according to Jeffrey Bland, Ph.D., president of the Northwest Academy of Preventive Medicine. Margarine contains by-products of the hydrogenation process that may actually promote increased blood cholesterol levels, even though the margarines themselves have no cholesterol in them.

Polyunsaturated Oils

Safflower, sunflower, soy, corn, canola (rapeseed), and linseed or flax seed oils are the most common polyunsaturated oils. They provide the 3 primary fatty acids—linoleic, linolenic, and arachidonic. These are called essential because they cannot be produced in the body, but serve many important bodily functions. They are essential for the regulation of a class of hormones called *prostaglandins* and are extremely important for the stimulation of the developing nervous system. It has been found that a fatty acid deficiency leads to a suppressed immune system, which can make us more vulnerable to disease.

Because linseed is the most polyunsaturated of all the oils, it is the kind I use to make Healthy Heart Butter. It has such a low melting point that it remains liquid when frozen and can be used directly from the freezer. It is found in cold water fish such as mackerel and salmon. It can be added to fruit juice and to cereals. I like to add it to peanut butter; it makes it more spreadable without affecting the flavor. It can also be added to the syrup used on pancakes and waffles, and makes an excellent salad dressing oil.

CLARIFYING CHOLESTEROL

There is increasing evidence that elevated cholesterol is associated with increased risk of heart disease. The consensus is that for every 1 percent that you lower your serum cholesterol, you will decrease your risk of dying from a heart attack by 2 percent.

A cholesterol level of 200 or lower is classified as "desirable" by the National Heart, Lung, and Blood Institute. From 200 to 239 is "borderline"; from 240 to 260, "moderate risk"; and beyond that "high risk."

If you have an elevated cholesterol, it does not necessarily mean that you are consuming too much cholesterol. Your elevated cholesterol may be the result of total dietary fat consumed—especially the saturated type—and may come from eating excessive animal protein, insufficient fiber, too much sugar, and from imbalances of vitamins or minerals. Or it can be the result of a lack of exercise or of being overweight. Or it could be from emotional stress.

Edward R. Pinckney, M.D., points out that cholesterol levels increase in response to some emotional situations. In one series of experiments, the cholesterol levels of medical students shot up immediately after an examination was announced. Soldiers have shown elevated cholesterol levels when required to perform a dangerous mission.

But don't let "cholesterol mania" take the joy out of eating! Remember that some cholesterol is necessary, even beneficial. The body uses it as a major constituent of cell membranes. It is an essential component of most body tissues, especially those of the brain and nervous system. It is needed to form sex and adrenal hormones, vitamin D, and bile, which is needed for the digestion of fats.

Good and Bad Cholesterol

Those people who have the lowest incidence of heart disease are those who have very high levels of HDL (high-density lipoprotein). This is the "good" cholesterol, which acts like a vacuum cleaner, sweeping through the bloodstream, picking up cholesterol and facilitating its elimination from the body through its conversion to bile.

The "bad" cholesterols are the LDLs, and to some extent the VLDLs (low-density and very low-density lipoproteins). They work their mischief by depositing fatty materials on the arterial walls, while the HDLs prevent cholesterol from being deposited and hasten its removal.

Recent evidence indicates that when the ratio of a person's total blood cholesterol to HDL is 5:1, that individual has a normal risk of heart disease. When the total cholesterol to HDL ratio is 8:1, there is twice the risk, and when the ratio is 4:1, only half the normal risk.

Let's say you have a total cholesterol of 240 and an HDL of 60. congratulations: Your ratio is 4:1. You have only half the normal risk of heart disease. Suppose your total cholesterol is 240 and your HDL is only 30. Your ratio is 8:1, or twice the risk. Go right to the chapter on "Bless-Your-Heart Smart Breakfasts." Stock up on beans, oat bran, lecithin granules, olive or canola oil, fruits, vegetables, nuts, and seeds. These are the foods that have been shown to lower total cholesterol and improve HDL levels.

Now let's look at your LDL, which is a more certain indicator of cholesterol risk. If LDL is above 160, the situation is defined as high risk. If the LDL is from 130 to 159, the situation needs attention but the risk is not as great. You can reduce your LDL by cutting back on saturated fats and by eliminating caffeine, sugar, white flour, cigarettes, and alcohol. Increase your consumption of the foods listed above that raise HDL levels.

When It's All in the Family

There are some people who have a genetic problem called *hypercholesterolemia*, an inherited tendency to elevated cholesterol and cardiovascular problems. No matter how they adjust their diets and lifestyles, their livers are unable to maintain safe cholesterol levels.

Dr. William Connor of the University of Oregon School of Medicine has used high doses of niacin (Vitamin B₃) on patients with this familial trait and achieved remarkable reductions in cholesterol levels—averaging 20 to 30 percent lower levels. The dosage is high—1,000 to 2,000 milligrams 2 to 3 times a day. You must start slowly with niacin because it causes flushing and itching skin. This effect passes in about half an hour. High doses over an extended period can cause nausea, in which case, back off. Niacin therapy should be tried only under your physician's supervision, but you can get more niacin in your diet. Good sources of niacin are wheat bran, buckwheat, wheat germ, peanuts, soy beans, whole wheat flours, almonds, sunflower and sesame seeds, eggs, and milk.

Smart Breakfasts includes many foods that are rich in niacin and other nutrients that have been shown to lower total cholesterol levels and increase HDLs.

THE ESSENTIAL FRUIT

A good starting point for a smart breakfast is fruit. If you have been starting your day with a glass of orange juice, try switching to the whole fruit. You'll get more fiber, more of the very important bioflavonoids which help keep capillary walls strong. And all this with fewer calories—1 cup of orange juice provides about 112 calories; a whole medium-size orange provides only 62 calories. Eat the whole orange, including the white inner rind that is still attached to the fruit segments.

I make it a regular morning practice to put on the table a plate of cut-up oranges, with the pith left on and the outer rind removed. Everybody digs in while assembling breakfast or while waiting to be served. It's also a good idea to prepare a bowl of fresh fruit salad in the evening and refrigerate it overnight. Topped with yogurt or cottage cheese and some oat bran crunch or granola, this makes a great rush-hour breakfast.

The orange rind, usually discarded, contains minerals, vitamins, bioflavonoids, fiber, and wonderful flavor. The inner white rind is a storehouse of bioflavonoids. Neither of these parts of the orange should be discarded. Both should be used. Here's how you can make use of the whole orange:

Try to get organically grown fruit, which is available at most health food stores. If you can't find organically raised fruit, then give your fruit a 15-minute bath in a basin of water with about ¼ cup vinegar in it. Then scrub the orange with soapy water, using a stiff brush, and rinse it several times, until there is no hint of the soap. Wipe it dry. The idea is to minimize the amount of pesticides applied in the growing process.

With a vegetable peeler, peel off the thin layer of orange rind. Place it on paper toweling and allow it to dry. It will dry quickly at room temperature and even more quickly when placed on a radiator or in a warm—not hot—oven. When it is dry, pulverize it into a coarse powder and store it in a small jar with a perforated lid, such as an unused salt shaker.

If the white pith is not consumed, dry it the same way as the rind. Pulverize it and place it in another container of the same kind. Use these powders whenever a recipe in *Smart Breakfasts* calls for grated orange rind.

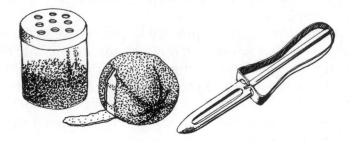

1

THE NEW HERO
ON THE MENU
Fiber-Rich Hot and Cold Cereals

Oatmeal Cookie Crunch Cereal
Maple Walnut Oatmeal
Miraculous Steel-Cut Oats
Energy-Replenishing Buckwheat
Orange Bulgur with Pistachios
Incredible Creamy Quinoa
Almond Crunch Granola
Dr. Rinse's Breakfast Mash
Dynamite Wheat Germ Cereal

Now that the fear of cholesterol has chased bacon and eggs off the breakfast table, cereal has taken the place of honor on the menu. And rightfully so. Both hot and cold cereals provide powerhouse nutrients, the kind we all need to charge our batteries in the morning. They are high in complex carbohydrates for sustained energy, provide protein, minerals, and B-complex vitamins. They are also very low in fat and very high in fiber. Because fiber in the morning starts your day off on the right foot, we have included a fiber count with each of the recipes in this chapter.

For many of us, it is the aroma of oatmeal simmering on the back burner that triggers fond memories. But oatmeal has a lot more than nostalgia going for it. Long before oat bran got rave reviews for its ability to reduce serum cholesterol levels, oatmeal demonstrated a striking ability to lower cholesterol. You can further increase the cholesterol-lowering power of your oatmeal if you add two tablespoons of oat bran to each portion of oatmeal as it is cooking. In this way, you get all the many wonder-working features of the whole grain (which oat bran lacks) as well as a boost of extra bran.

Compared to other grains, oats have the highest protein content and the highest-quality protein. True, oat protein is slightly deficient in the amino acids lysine, methionine, and threonine, but you're not expected to live on oats alone. Eat your oatmeal with milk or yogurt, or cook the oatmeal with soy grits. Both dairy products and legumes are high in lysine. Nuts and seeds are high in methionine and threonine.

To avoid boredom at the breakfast table, vary the grains you serve. Variety not only sparks appetites, it provides a wider range of nutrients. According to an old Japanese proverb, every time you eat a new food, you add 75 days to your life.

Oatmeal Cookie Crunch Cereal

This oatmeal has a delicious sweetness that everyone will love. The raisins, added first, sweeten the water in which the oats are cooked. The nuts and seeds give it a crunchy quality, as well as making this dish a complete protein.

2 cups water	½ teaspoon vanilla
½ cup raisins	¼ cup sunflower seeds
1 cup rolled oats	¼ cup chopped walnuts
½ teaspoon cinnamon	

In a 1-quart saucepan, combine water and raisins. Bring to a boil. Add oats gradually, stirring. Add cinnamon and vanilla. Reduce heat and cook for about 8 minutes. Ladle into bowls and top with seeds and nuts, or offer the seeds and nuts on the side. Children like to help themselves to the extras. Serve with milk, cream, or yogurt.

Note: Make the full amount even though you may be cooking for only one or two. Refrigerate or freeze the uneaten oatmeal in single-portion containers. When you want to microwave a quick breakfast, you've got it made.

Microwave Method *(settings on high, except where noted)*

In a 2-quart casserole, combine all ingredients. Mix well. Micro-cook on high for 8 to 10 minutes, depending on consistency desired. Stir after half the time.

Yield: Makes 4 servings.

Each serving provides: 184 calories (cal), 5.5 grams (g) protein (pro), 1.7 g saturated (sat) fat, 4 g unsaturated (unsat) fat, 6.1 g fiber.

Maple Walnut Oatmeal

Oatmeal can be paired with fruits and nuts in uncountable combinations. This combination is my grandson's favorite. He says it's almost as good as an ice-cream cone.

1½ cups water
⅔ cup rolled oats
2 tablespoons wheat germ

2 tablespoons chopped walnuts
1 tablespoon pure maple syrup

In a saucepan, combine the water and the oats. Bring to a boil, then reduce heat and simmer for 2 minutes. Stir in the wheat germ, nuts, and maple syrup. Cook for another 2 minutes or until the oatmeal is the desired consistency.

Microwave Method
Combine all ingredients in a 4-cup glass measure. Stir thoroughly. Microcook on high 3 to 4 minutes, depending on consistency desired. Watch carefully. Oatmeal tends to boil over.
Yield: Makes 3 servings.
Each serving provides: 82 cal, 4 g pro, 2 g fat, 4 g fiber.

Miraculous Steel-Cut Oats

Steel-cut oats are made by cutting the oat groats into small pieces with steel rollers. Long a mainstay of the Irish, it is now the Cadillac of the oatmeal family, rarely enjoyed because it requires long cooking. Microwave cooking should bring it back to the breakfast menu.

> 1 cup water
> 1/3 cup steel-cut oats

In a saucepan, combine water and oats. Bring to a boil, lower heat slightly, and cook for 40 to 50 minutes, stirring occasionally. Or, to avoid stirring and prevent sticking, use a double boiler.

Microwave Method
Combine water and oats in a 4-cup glass measure. Cover tightly with microwave plastic wrap and microcook on high for 6 minutes. Pierce the plastic with the tip of a knife to let steam escape, then remove the plastic and microcook uncovered for 3 minutes.
Yield: Makes 2 servings.
Each serving provides: 65 cal, 2.4 g pro, 1 g fat, 4 g fiber.

Variation:
Add raisins or prunes.

Energy-Replenishing Buckwheat

If you want to turn your thermostat down and your body heat up, have a steaming bowl of buckwheat groats for breakfast. Unlike other cereal grains, buckwheat has a high lysine content. It is rich in vitamin E, the whole family of B vitamins, and has twice as much calcium as other grains. Buckwheat is a distinguished member of the rhubarb family and not a true grain. It can, therefore, be enjoyed by those who are allergic to grains. You'll find more recipes for buckwheat and other grains in the "Smart Breakfasts for the Allergic" chapter.

1 cup buckwheat groats	¼ teaspoon salt or
2 cups water	vegetable seasoning (optional)

Sprinkle buckwheat into boiling water. Stir for 1 minute. Reduce heat to simmer, cover pot, and cook for about 10 minutes.

Serve with yogurt or milk and fruit, and a bit of honey.

Microwave Method

In a 4-cup glass measure, combine ½ cup buckwheat groats and 2 cups of water. Stir. Microcook on high for 5 minutes.

Yield: Makes 4 servings.

Each serving, without topping, provides: 81 cal, 3 g pro, .6 g fat, 8.4 g fiber.

Variation:

For a creamy consistency, cook 1 cup buckwheat kernels in 5 cups of water or a combination of water and milk.

Orange Bulgur with Pistachios

Bulgur, a popular Middle Eastern staple, is made from whole wheat berries that have been steamed, then dried and crushed. It is quick cooking and has a pleasant, nutty flavor.

2 cups orange juice or
1 cup water and 1 cup
   orange juice
1 cup bulgur

¼ cup chopped pistachios
   (almonds may be
   substituted)

In a saucepan bring the orange juice or the combination of orange juice and water to a boil. Add the bulgur and cook over lowered heat for 10 to 15 minutes. Add the nuts, or pass them at the table.

Microwave Method
In a 4-cup glass measure, combine the juice and water. Stir in the bulgur. Cover with plastic wrap and microcook on high for 2 minutes and 20 seconds. Uncover and cook for 1 more minute. Remove from oven and let stand for 1 minute.
Yield: Makes 3 servings.
Each serving with pistachios provides: 270 cal, 7 g pro, 3 g unsat fat, 7.2 g fiber.

Incredible Creamy Quinoa

Not really a grain, but a member of the goosefoot family, quinoa (pronounced keen-wa), dates back to the Incas, who called it the "Mother Grain." Beets, chard, and spinach are also members of the goosefoot family, so called because their triangular leaves resemble the webbed foot of a goose. Quinoa is high in lysine, which vegetables and most grains are deficient in, provides fiber, minerals, vitamin E, and the morale-boosting B vitamins. It has a pleasant translucence, reminiscent of tapioca, and marries well with all kinds of fruits.

1 cup quinoa
2 cups water
1 apple, unpeeled and thinly
sliced

¼ cup raisins
½ teaspoon cinnamon

Put the quinoa in a strainer and rinse it thoroughly. In a large saucepan, combine the quinoa and water and bring to a boil. Cover and cook for 5 minutes. Add the apples, raisins, and cinnamon and simmer until water is absorbed (about 10 minutes).

Microwave Method
Combine the rinsed quinoa and water in a 4-cup glass measure. Cover tightly with microwave plastic and microcook on high for 5 minutes. Uncover and stir. Add the apple, raisins, and cinnamon. Microcook for 5 more minutes or until water is absorbed.
Yield: Makes 5 servings.
Each serving provides: 150 cal, 5.4 g pro, 2 g unsat fat, 6.4 g fiber.

Almond Crunch Granola

This recipe is sweet and crunchy, even though it has no added sweeteners and no added fat. Adults and children will love it, and it's a breakfast that anyone can easily and quickly assemble.

½ cup raisins
1 cup hot water or unsweetened apple juice
3 cups uncooked rolled oats
1 cup shredded coconut,
 unsweetened
½ cup sesame seeds
½ cup sunflower seeds
½ cup soy nuts, flakes, or
 grits

¼ cup dry milk powder
½ cup wheat germ
¼ cup wheat bran
¼ cup oat bran
1 teaspoon cinnamon
½ cup chopped or sliced
 almonds

Preheat oven to 250°F.

Soak the raisins in the water or juice for a few hours, or overnight.

In a large bowl, combine all of the dry ingredients. Pour the water or juice from the soaking raisins into a cup. Pour this liquid over the oat mixture and mix to moisten the grains. Spread this mixture on two cookie sheets lined with parchment paper or sprayed with no-stick baking spray. Bake for 1 hour stirring the mixture every 15 minutes. Add the soaked raisins, turn off the heat, and let the mixture sit in the oven for another 15 minutes. It should be dry and crackly by then. If it isn't, leave it in the oven a little longer with the heat on.

Remove from oven and let it cool. Store in tightly lidded containers—such as Mason jars. Keep it refrigerated or frozen. It can be used directly from the freezer.

Serve with milk or yogurt.

Add fruit in season.

Microwave Method

Place raisins and juice in a bowl, loosely covered, then in the microwave, on high, for 2 minutes. Follow instructions above, but place parchment or wax paper on the bottom of the microwave oven. Spread about half the dampened granola in a single layer and microcook on high for 2 minutes. Add half the raisins and microcook for 10 seconds. Repeat for the second batch. Cool and store as above.

Yield: Makes 2 quarts.

Each ¼ portion provides: 80 cal, 5 g pro, 1 g sat fat, 2 g unsat fat, 6 g fiber.

Dr. Rinse's Breakfast Mash

This is a form of muesli developed by Dr. Jacobus Rinse, a Dutch chemist, who at a fairly young age suffered a heart attack and was told to take it easy or he wouldn't last another 10 years. He ate this concoction every morning, took extra vitamin E and C, and at the age of 80 was busily building a log cabin. This muesli can be enjoyed solo or in combination with other dry cereals or as a topping on a hot cereal.

1 cup rolled oats
1 cup bran
1 cup wheat germ
¼ cup lecithin granules

¼ cup sunflower seeds
1 tablespoon sesame seeds
1 tablespoon brewer's yeast
1 teaspoon bone meal

In a large bowl, mix together all ingredients. Ladle into a jar with a tight-fitting cover and store in the refrigerator or freezer. Serve with milk, yogurt, or fruit juice, topped with raisins, chopped apple, sliced bananas, or chopped nuts.

Yield: Makes 1 quart or 8 servings.

Each serving provides: 116 cal, 6 g pro, 4 g unsat fat, 5.4 g fiber.

Dynamite Wheat Germ Cereal

Wheat germ, the heart or embryo of the wheat grain, is a power-house of nutrients. It contains an unusually large amount of vitamin E in addition to generous amounts of every member of the vitamin B family, and lots of potassium, magnesium, zinc, and iron—the organic kind that does not fight with vitamin E.

Keep your wheat germ refrigerated or frozen. If you use raw wheat germ, buy from a dealer who keeps it under refrigeration. Raw wheat germ has more nutrients than the toasted kind because it has not been subjected to heat, while the toasted has better keeping qualities and a flavor that is more acceptable to some palates. To give raw wheat germ a toasty flavor, toast about ½ cup in a 250°F oven until light brown and add to the rest of the jar. The whole jar of wheat germ will then taste toasted. Or roast some raw peanuts along with the wheat germ. You will improve the flavor of both.

6 tablespoons toasted wheat germ
1 cup milk or ½ cup yogurt

1 sliced banana, or sliced peaches or strawberries, in season

This is a do-it-yourself cereal. Get a bowl and a spoon, sit down, and eat.

Yield: Makes 1 serving.

Each serving with bananas provides: 219 cal, 1 g pro, 2 g sat fat, 2.5 g unsat fat, 6.5 g fiber.

2
THE GOOD EGG
Baked, Shirred, Steamed, Coddled; in Omelets and Soufflés

Who does not remember the breakfasts of yesteryear—the fluffy omelets and soufflés, the sunny sides, once-over-lightly, or poached eggs, with firm whites and runny yolks? These foods made breakfast a time of replenishing the spirit as well as the body.

And no wonder! The egg, a biological structure designed by Mother Nature for the reproduction of the chicken, is one of the most nutritious and versatile of foods. Nothing else, except mother's milk, gives us everything we need in terms of protein, vitamins, and minerals. Eggs are one of the few foods that can support life entirely on their own. A serving of 2 eggs provides about 14 grams of the highest-quality protein, plus 12 grams of fat, 1 gram of carbohydrate, at least 13 minerals and 13 vitamins—all for only 160 calories. (A large egg has only 80 calories, 60 of which are in the yolk.) As much as 12 percent of the egg is protein, and every bit of that protein is digested and put to use in your body.

If eggs are so wholesome, why do so many doctors caution against them? Because egg yolks are one of the richest sources of cholesterol in the American diet, and the American Heart Association recommends that we limit cholesterol intake to no more than 300 milligrams a day. One egg yolk provides about 275 milligrams.

But some researchers have questioned the wisdom of this black-balling of the egg, because while high in cholesterol, eggs *don't* raise blood cholesterol or triglycerides, according to many studies.

Even the AHA Dietary Goals acknowledge that foods high in saturated fat (eggs are not) are a greater risk than high-cholesterol foods, and advise that for children, the elderly, and pre-menopausal women, eggs have more benefits than risks.

Consider also that lecithin, by emulsifying cholesterol, dislodges it from blood vessels. Eggs are said to contain *8 times* as much lecithin as cholesterol.

What, then, should we do about eggs? Some doctors who practice nutritional medicine advise 2 eggs a day, even for patients with elevated cholesterol. Other, more orthodox, physicians, many of whom have very little background in nutrition, advise patients with heart disease or a family history of it to avoid eggs altogether.

Many of the recipes in this chapter include foods rich in niacin and other nutrients that have been shown to lower total cholesterol levels and increase HDL, the good cholesterol. If you have been strongly advised against egg yolks, you might try using 2 whites for every yolk in the recipes in this chapter.

EGG DOS AND DON'TS

- No matter how hurried you are in the morning, never hurry the cooking of the eggs. Cook at a low to moderate heat. The term "boiled eggs" is actually a misnomer. Eggs should never be boiled. High temperatures toughen the eggs and diminish the fresh taste.
- Eggs should be purchased from refrigerated display cases and should be refrigerated promptly when you get home, large end up.
- Only fresh, clean, unbroken eggs should be used when making milk shakes and other uncooked or lightly cooked dishes.
- The thick, rope-like strands of white on opposite sides of the yolk, called the chalazae (ka-LAY-zee), anchor the yolks as the egg develops and are an indicator of freshness. As eggs mature, the chalazae disappear.
- Eggs can be stored in their carton in the refrigerator for at least 4 to 5 weeks. Hard-cooked eggs should be stored in the refrigera-

tor as soon as they are cool and should be used within a week. Raw whites keep a week to 10 days if refrigerated in a tightly covered container. Refrigerate unbroken raw yolks, covered with water, in a tightly covered container. Drain and use within 2 to 3 days.

- For hard-cooked eggs you should use your oldest eggs because very fresh eggs may be harder to peel when hard cooked.
- Store eggs away from strong-smelling foods since they readily absorb odors.
- A pretty and edible garnish always enhances the pleasure of eating eggs. Use sprigs of parsley or watercress, a slice of Bermuda onion or a scallion, a slice of avocado, tomato, or orange, or toasted chopped almonds. I like to serve scallions, chives, or chopped onions with eggs for two reasons: First, the sharp contrasting flavor enhances the rich mellow flavor of the egg and makes salt unnecessary; perhaps more important, it has been shown that the *onion family, both raw and cooked, is a cholesterol fighter.*

How to Cook an Egg

Eggs can be prepared in thousands of ways. If you're counting calories, the simpler the better.

HARD- AND SOFT-COOKED EGGS
Put the eggs in a saucepan with cold water to cover. Bring the water just to a boil, then reduce the heat to simmer. For soft-cooked eggs, simmer for 3 to 5 minutes depending on how firm you like the whites. When the eggs are done, pour out the boiling water, and set

the pot under cold running water for a few seconds to cool them enough so you can handle them. A properly done soft-cooked egg will have a slightly moist, tender white and a runny yolk. Serve hot on toast or with pieces of toast, oat bran crunch, or chopped scallions or chives sprinkled on top.

For hard-cooked eggs, simmer for 10 to 15 minutes, then plunge into cold water immediately to stop the cooking. If you do not cool them immediately, the whites stick to the shell, making them difficult to peel. Also the iron in the yolk combines with the sulfur in the white, resulting in an unappetizing green ring around the yolk.

CODDLED EGGS

Bring a pot of water to a boil. While the water is heating set the eggs in a bowl of warm water. (This will prevent the eggs from cracking when immersed in the boiling water.) With a tablespoon, carefully lower the eggs into the pot of water. Cover the pan and remove from the heat. For soft-coddled eggs, let them stand for 3 to 5 minutes. For hard-coddled eggs, 10 to 15 minutes.

STEAMED EGGS

Put about 1½ inches of water in the bottom of the steamer pan. Bring the water to a boil. Place eggs on a steamer rack and place rack in the steamer pan. Lower heat to simmer. For soft-steamed eggs simmer for 3 to 5 minutes. For hard-steamed eggs, simmer for 10 to 15 minutes.

POACHED EGGS

Poached eggs have a wonderful delicate flavor. Unlike fried eggs, they're prepared with no added fat, so they're very low in calories. They're also quickly prepared. Use the freshest eggs available and they will poach into lovely spheres with high round yolks. You could use a poaching ring to keep them in neat rounds or an egg poacher, which is really an egg steamer. I prefer the following method:

Put enough water in a shallow pan to cover the eggs. Bring the water to a boil. Break one egg or more into a platter. Swirl the boiling water with a wooden spoon to make a whirlpool and slip the eggs into it. (It is not necessary to add salt, vinegar, or lemon juice to hasten the coagulation of the white as suggested in many cookbooks.) Let the water cool to simmer, cover the pan, and let eggs remain there for 3 to 5 minutes. Remove eggs with a slotted spoon. Serve on toast, English muffins, a bed of baked potatoes, spinach, or cottage cheese.

Variation:
Use chicken broth or milk as the poaching liquid.

Microwave Method
Put ¼ cup of water in a 6-ounce custard cup. Break and slip the egg into the water. Prick the yolk with the tip of a knife, just enough to pierce the outer membrane. Microcook on high for 45 seconds to 1 minute.

BAKED EGGS
One of the easiest ways to prepare tender, flavorful eggs is to *bake* them. Even the children get perfect results by this method. Break eggs into lightly buttered custard cups or muffin tins. Place the containers in a pan of hot water and cover with parchment paper. Bake at 325°F until the whites are milky and the yolks are soft—about 5 minutes. Remove while still soft since the containers hold enough heat to continue cooking for a few seconds.

Variation:

You don't have to stick to baking cups. Try baked-potato shells, scooped-out tomatoes, a bed of spinach, cooked macaroni, brown rice or beans.

SHIRRED EGGS

Shirred eggs combine the techniques of frying and baking, and are very easy to make.

In a lightly buttered ovenproof dish, crack and cook the eggs on top of the stove until the whites just start to set. Transfer the dish to a 325°F oven and bake for about 5 minutes.

STEAM-FRIED EGGS

You can have perfect sunny-side-ups without the usual grease. Here's how: Use only enough butter, oil, or Healthy Heart Butter (see index) to keep the eggs from sticking on the bottom of a heavy skillet—about ¼ to ½ teaspoon. Warm over low heat until a few drops of water sprinkled in the pan do a lively dance. Break the eggs one at a time into a saucer and slide them into the skillet, being careful to keep them separate. For each egg, add 1 tablespoon of water or broth. Cover tightly and cook until the whites are set—2 to 3 minutes.

If you like your eggs "over-easy," use a spatula to turn them over very gently for the last few seconds of cooking.

SCRAMBLED EGGS

The secret to soft, fluffy, scrambled eggs is gentle heat. Beat the eggs with a fork, a whisk, or in a blender. Add 1 tablespoon of liquid for every 2 eggs. The liquid can be water, milk, or broth. If you like your eggs a solid golden yellow, beat thoroughly. For a combination of yellow and white flecks, blend lightly. For the greatest volume and airy lightness, beat the whites separately.

For best results, use an 8-inch skillet for 4 eggs. Heat 1 table-spoon butter in the skillet and reduce heat to low. Blend or mix together 4 eggs and 2 tablespoons water, milk, or broth. Pour the egg mixture into the pan. As the eggs begin to cook, stir to keep them from sticking to the pan and to let the uncooked portion flow to the bottom. When they hold their shape but are still moist and slightly undercooked—after about 2 to 3 minutes—remove from heat. They will continue to cook for a few seconds after they are removed from the burner. Pile them immediately onto warmed plates. Garnish with parsley, scallion, or chives, or a slice of onion topped with a slice of tomato.

Microwave Method

In a 9-inch pie plate, melt the butter on high, about 30 seconds. Pour in the egg mixture and cover with lid or plastic wrap. Cook 1 minute on high. Using a rubber spatula or wooden spoon, break up cooked portions and push toward center. Cover and cook 1 minute more. Stir again, cover, and let stand 1 minute more to finish cooking.

Mushroom and Onion Scramble

You get a lot of good eating for very few calories in this quickly prepared dish of tender scrambled eggs.

1 tablespoon butter	1 cup chopped mushrooms
½ cup chopped onion	8 eggs
½ cup chopped celery	¼ cup grated Parmesan cheese

In a large skillet, melt the butter and slightly sauté the onions, celery, and mushrooms. Beat the eggs and cheese together. Pour the egg mixture over the vegetables. As the eggs begin to cook, stir to keep them from sticking to the pan and to let the uncooked portion flow to the bottom. When they hold their shape but are still moist and slightly undercooked, in about 4 minutes, remove from heat. They will continue to cook for a few seconds. Pile them immediately onto heated plates.

Microwave Method

You save on cleanup when you cook your eggs in the dish they're served in. In a 1½-quart dish, combine the onions and celery. Cook 2 minutes on high. Top with mushrooms. Beat together the eggs and cheese. Pour the egg mixture over the vegetables and cover with lid or plastic wrap. Cook 3 minutes on high. With a rubber spatula or wooden spoon, break up the cooked portions and push toward the center. Cook 2 to 3 minutes more, breaking up mixture once or twice, until set, but before eggs reach desired doneness. Stir again, cover, and let stand 2 to 3 minutes to finish cooking. Spoon into warm plates.

Yield: Makes 4 servings.

Each serving provides: 230 cal, 19 g pro, 8 g sat fat, 7 g unsat fat.

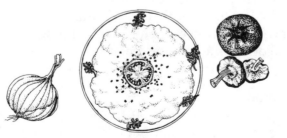

Omelets—Plain and Fluffy

PLAIN

Omelets are quick, versatile, and, when properly made, heavenly. Every omelet has 3 basic ingredients—eggs, a liquid, and butter to cook it in. Salt toughens an omelet. Enhance the flavor of the eggs with chives, dill, parsley, marjoram, pepper, and thyme in small amounts, individually or in combination. Use a heavy-bottomed skillet with sloping sides. Small omelets cook so quickly that it's easy to custom-make them to order. Omelets are the exception to the rule that eggs should be cooked at low temperature.

3 eggs	1/4 teaspoon dried thyme
2 to 3 tablespoons water,	dash of pepper
milk, or fruit juice	1 teaspoon butter

In a small bowl, beat the eggs, seasonings, and liquid only until there are no visible lumps—about 30 beats.

Heat the butter in the pan until it is bubbly but not until it browns. Pour the egg mixture in the pan. Use a spatula or a fork to draw the edges toward the center and tilt the pan to let the uncooked portion flow underneath. Cook until the top is moist but not runny—about 30 seconds. If you want to add a filling, spread it on half of the omelet. (See the following recipes for omelet fillings.) Fold the omelet in half as you slide it onto a heated plate.

Microwave Method

In a 9-inch pie plate melt the butter on high, about 45 seconds. Spread the butter to cover the bottom of the plate. Mix the remaining ingredients as described above and pour into the plate. Cover tightly with plastic wrap and cook on high 2 to 3 minutes, preferably on a micro-turntable or by rotating ¼ turn each 30 seconds. Do not stir. When center is set but still moist, add filling if desired. Fill the omelet when it is slightly underdone because the heat retained in the eggs completes the cooking. (See the following recipes for omelet fillings.) With a spatula, fold the omelet in half and slide it from the pie plate onto a warm serving plate.

If you're using a microwave browning dish, preheat the browning dish on high for 1 minute. Add butter and spread to coat the bottom. Pour in the egg mixture and cover with lid. Cook on high 1½ to 2 minutes, on a turntable or by rotating ¼ turn every 30 seconds. For repeated use, wipe out dish and preheat each time about 30 seconds. **Yield:** Makes 2 servings.
Each serving provides: 135 cal, 10 g pro, 5.5 g sat fat, 6 g unsat fat.

FLUFFY OMELET
Fluffy omelets are cooked in two stages. First, you partially cook the omelet, then you bake it uncovered in a 350°F. oven. Make sure the skillet you are using is ovenproof.

2 eggs, separated	*¼ teaspoon cream of tartar*
¼ teaspoon vegetable seasoning	*1 teaspoon butter*
1 tablespoon water	

Beat the egg whites and yolks separately. Beat the yolks with the seasoning to a thick yellow foam and the whites with water and cream of tartar until soft peaks form. Immediately fold the yolks into the whites by the following method: First, spoon the yolks over the whites; next, with a spatula, gently spread the yolks; then lift the whites from the bottom and gently turn them over the yolks. Do this until there are no streaks of white or yellow.

Preheat oven to 350°F. Heat the butter in an ovenproof skillet until it is bubbly but not brown. Pour the egg mixture immediately into the skillet and cook the same as a plain omelet until the bottom is set but the top is still moist. Switch it to the preheated oven for a few minutes. When it looks puffy, test it for doneness by touching the surface lightly. If it springs back and looks slightly dry, it is ready. Remove it from the oven, fold it in half, and slip it onto a warm plate. Enjoy!

Microwave Method

To enhance the color and texture, use the microwave browning dish for this recipe.

In large mixing bowl, beat egg whites with water and cream of tartar at high speed until soft peaks form. In a small bowl, beat the egg yolks and seasonings until thick and lemon-colored. Gently fold yolks into whites as described above. Preheat the browning dish on high for 1½ minutes. Add butter and spread to coat the bottom of the dish. Pour in the egg mixture and smooth the surface with a spatula. Cook on high for 1 to 1½ minutes or until top is set. With spatula, turn omelet over in dish and let stand 1 minute. Slide omelet from the browning dish onto a warm serving plate. If desired, spoon your choice of filling over the top and serve immediately. (See the following recipes for omelet fillings.)

Yield: Makes 1 serving.

Each serving provides: 191 cal, 13 g pro, 8 g sat fat, 7.5 g unsat fat.

Omelet Fillings

When it comes to fillings for omelets, the sky is the limit. Fillings can be sweet or savory, substantial or light. Use ¼ to ⅓ cup filling for a 4-egg omelet; ½ cup filling for a 6- to 8-egg omelet. Fillings should be added during the last few seconds of cooking, when the top is moist but not runny. Spread the filling over half the omelet, fold the omelet in half, and remove from heat.

You can also use a spoonful of filling as a topping.

Here are some suggested fillings:

1. Any cooked vegetables, chopped, diced, or sliced.
2. Shredded or sliced cheddar, Swiss, Muenster, mozzarella, or any firm cheese, preferably part skim.
3. Ricotta, cottage, or cream cheese or yogurt creamless cream cheese (see index for recipe).
4. Cooked and crumbled ground beef.
5. Sautéed mushrooms, chopped onions, green or red peppers.
6. Chopped nuts and seeds.
7. Unsweetened fruit conserves.
8. Drained crushed pineapple.
9. Yogurt mixed with wheat germ and oat bran.
10. Chicken livers, chopped and cooked with onions.
11. Drained and flaked tuna or any cooked fish.

(There is no need to heat cheese, nuts, jelly, or jam.)

Herbed Asparagus Omelet

Every bite of this omelet tastes like a celebration of spring. Asparagus provides so many vital nutrients that can put spring in your stride. It's a good source of vitamins A, B complex, C, and E, potassium, and zinc. It also provides rutin, a bioflavonoid which strengthens capillary membranes, thus preventing rupturing of the blood vessels.

4 stalks asparagus
1 teaspoon butter or oil
1/4 cup mushrooms, thinly
    sliced
1 teaspoon tamari soy sauce
1 teaspoon dried basil
2 eggs
1 tablespoon water

1 tablespoon fresh parsley,
    minced
1/8 teaspoon freshly grated
    nutmeg
1 teaspoon butter
    minced fresh parsley for
    garnish

To make the filling: Cut the asparagus into 1-inch pieces and steam them, tightly covered, until tender, about 5 minutes. Set aside.

Heat 1 tablespoon butter or oil in a small skillet. Add the sliced mushrooms, tamari, and basil, and stir. Cook mushrooms about 4 minutes or until tender, stirring occasionally. Stir in the asparagus.

To make the omelet: Using a fork, beat the eggs and water together until light, about 20 strokes. Stir in the minced parsley and nutmeg. Place an omelet pan over medium heat and add the butter. When the butter melts, add the egg mixture and swirl the pan to distribute the egg evenly. Continue to swirl the pan as you stir the top layer of egg with a fork, and pull the cooked edges of the omelet toward the center of the pan, allowing the uncooked portion to run toward the edges of the pan where it will cook more quickly.

When the omelet is no longer runny but still moist on top, place the filling on half of the omelet. Fold the other half over it and turn the omelet out onto a serving plate. Garnish with fresh parsley.

Microwave Method

Place the cut asparagus on a plate, cover with plastic wrap, and microcook on high for 4 minutes. Set aside.

In an 8-inch pie plate, heat the butter or oil on high, uncovered for 1 minute. Add the mushrooms, tamari, and basil, cover and microcook on high for 2 minutes. Add to the asparagus mixture.

In the same plate, melt the teaspoon of butter on high for 1 minute, then add the beaten eggs, cover and microcook for 2 minutes. Let it set for 2 minutes, then add the filling as described above.
Yield: Makes 1 serving.
Each serving provides: 192 cal, 19 g pro, 7 g sat fat, 8 g unsat fat.

Royal Apricot Almond Soufflé

A soufflé is another version of the fluffy omelet except that it's made with sauce containing the egg yolks and is baked in a deep dish that permits it to rise to impressive heights. Soufflés welcome the same accompaniments as do omelets. This is a royal dish well worth the extra effort called for in its preparation.

2 teaspoons butter
½ cup finely ground toasted almonds
1 cup unsweetened apricot conserves
1 tablespoon lemon juice

1 tablespoon arrowroot
3 tablespoons honey
4 eggs, separated
¼ teaspoon cream of tartar
toasted slivered almonds for garnish

45

Preheat oven to 375°F. Butter bottom and sides of a 1½-quart soufflé dish and dust with ¼ cup finely ground almonds.

Combine remaining ingredients except egg whites and cream of tartar in blender or food processor, and whiz until light and fluffy.

In another bowl, beat egg whites until foamy. Add cream of tartar and continue beating until stiff peaks form. Fold about ¼ of the egg whites into the apricot mixture and blend well. Gently fold in the remaining egg whites.

Pour batter into prepared soufflé dish and bake for 25 to 30 minutes. Remove from oven and decorate with slivered almonds, and, for special occasions, with blobs of whipped cream.

Yield: Makes 4 to 6 servings.

Each of 4 servings provides: 364 cal, 11 g pro, 7 g sat fat, 7 g unsat fat.
Each of 6 servings provides: 239 cal, 9 g pro, 5 g sat fat, 5 g unsat fat.

Penthouse Cheese Soufflé

This Florentine soufflé is a delight to the senses.

¼ cup Healthy Heart Butter (see index for recipe)
¼ cup whole wheat flour
1¼ cups skim milk
¼ cup grated cheddar cheese

¼ cup cooked spinach, drained and chopped
3 eggs, separated
¼ teaspoon dried oregano

Preheat oven to 375°F.

Melt butter in saucepan. Stir in flour and cook for 1 minute. Remove from heat and gradually blend in milk. Heat, stirring until sauce thickens. Cook slightly. Then add cheese, spinach, egg yolk, and oregano. Mix thoroughly. Whisk egg whites until stiff and fold into cheese mixture.

Turn into greased 1-quart soufflé dish. Place in oven for 35 to 40 minutes or until well risen and golden brown. Serve immediately. **Yield:** Makes 4 servings.

Each serving provides: 296 cal, 16 g pro, 10 g sat fat, 8 g unsat fat.

Egg à la Pizza

Kids love this healthier version of their favorite food. So do their young-at-heart Pop-Pops and Grandmas. It's a typical pizza on top, with a slightly crunchy, cheese-flavored egg crust, flecked with green peppers.

1 tablespoon butter	½ teaspoon dried, crushed
1 small onion, chopped	oregano
½ small green pepper, chopped	¼ teaspoon dried, crushed
8 eggs, beaten	basil
½ cup milk, preferably skim	½ cup tomato sauce
½ cup lightly cooked mushrooms	1 ounce shredded, part-skim
¼ teaspoon pepper	mozzarella (¼ cup)

Preheat oven to 350°F.

In an ovenproof skillet, heat the butter until bubbly. Add the onion and green pepper and cook until onion is translucent—about 2 minutes.

In a mixing bowl, blend together the eggs, milk, mushrooms, and seasonings. Pour into the skillet. Cover and cook for about 6 or 7 minutes or until eggs are almost set, pushing cooked portions toward the center of the dish several times during the cooking.

Pour the tomato sauce over the eggs and sprinkle with cheese. Place the skillet in a 350°F oven or under a broiler for a few minutes or until the cheese melts. Cut into wedges.

Microwave Method

In an 8- or 9-inch round pie plate, cook the butter, uncovered, for 30 to 45 seconds or until melted. Add the onion and green pepper and cook, uncovered on high, for about 2 minutes or until vegetables are crisp, but tender.

In a mixing bowl, blend together the eggs, milk, mushrooms, and seasonings. Pour over the vegetables. Cook, uncovered, on high for 5 or 6 minutes or until eggs are almost set, pushing cooked portions to the center of the dish several times.

Pour tomato sauce over eggs and sprinkle with cheese. Cook on high for 1 to 1½ minutes or until cheese starts to melt.

Yield: Makes 4 to 6 servings.

Each serving for 4 provides: 240 cal, 14 g pro, 7 g sat fat, 6 g unsat fat.
Each serving for 6 provides: 160 cal, 9 g pro, 4.5 g sat fat, 3.5 g unsat fat.

Eggs in a Nest

This is a most unusual and amusing presentation, reminiscent of egg hunting down on the farm. It is also a very substantial stick-to-your-ribs meal. The sprouts bring the liveliness of springtime from the garden and provide chlorophyll, which has been shown to offer some protection against cancer. Both children and adults will love it.

> 4 slices toasted rye or whole
>   grain bread
> 2 cups chicken or tuna salad

> 2 cups alfalfa or mixed
>   sprouts
> 4 hard-cooked eggs

Spread a half cup of salad on each slice of toast. Top the salad with a handful of sprouts. Shape the sprouts to look like a little nest. Place a peeled, hard-cooked egg in the nest.
Yield: Makes 4 servings.
Each serving provides: 255 cal, 19 g pro, 13 g fat.

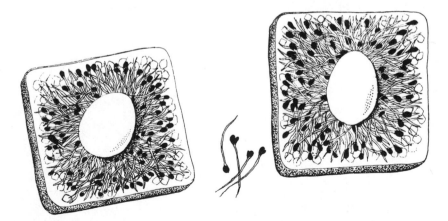

3

HEAVENLY, HEALTHY PANCAKES, WAFFLES, AND CREPES

Apple Cinnamon Walnut Pancakes
Rhode Island Johnnycakes
Zucchini Cheese Pancakes
Amaranth Yogurt Pancakes with Strawberry Sauce
Crunchy Potato Latkes
Buttermilk Maple Walnut Waffles
Orange Spice Popcorn Waffles
Oat Bran Waffles
Apple Blintzes with Raspberry Syrup
Orange Yogurt Crepes
Oat 'n' Cheese Blintzes
Tortillas

This category is usually the winner when kids vote on the breakfast menu. And that's fine with me. It means that instead of making eggs for some and cereal for others, I can incorporate the nutrients of both in one batter that pleases them all!

HOT TIPS FOR GREAT PANCAKES AND WAFFLES

Light, fluffy, and aromatic! Who can look at a stack of flapjacks or waffles and not feel elevated? Of course, when drowned in sugary syrup, they can be a nutritional disaster. But don't let the fear of syrup delete a whole category of eating pleasure. Make them with dynamite nutrients and serve them with toppings that are delicious and wholesome.

Here are some hot tips for better pancakes and waffles:

- Most batters can be used either on the griddle or in the waffle iron. However, for crispier waffles, add another egg and 2 additional tablespoons of shortening to the batter. Waffle batters, as a rule, have more flour than liquid ingredients.
- To make small pancakes uniform in size, drop the batter from a tablespoon. For large pancakes, use an ice-cream scoop or ¼-cup measure.
- To keep batter flowing smoothly, spray scoop or cup with nonstick cooking spray, or wipe with a mixture of liquid lecithin and oil.
- Always preheat the griddle or skillet.
- To test the readiness of the griddle, sprinkle with a few drops of water. If the water flattens and boils, the griddle is not hot enough. If it disappears at once, the griddle is too hot. If the drops do a bouncy jig, the griddle is ready.

- Nonstick griddles, skillets, and waffle irons need not be greased. Others should be brushed lightly with butter or oil or sprayed with nonstick cooking spray.
- Pancakes are usually ready to turn when they are covered with bubbles. Use a spatula to turn pancakes over to brown the other side. The second side will brown more quickly than the first.
- Place finished pancakes on a cookie sheet in a single layer and keep them warm in a 300°F oven.
- Unused pancake batter may be stored in the refrigerator, in a tightly covered container, for several days. Leftover pancakes can be refrigerated or frozen and then reheated in a toaster oven or microwave oven.
- If your waffle iron is brand new, follow manufacturer's directions for tempering.
- The waffle iron should be preheated for a few minutes or until it is hot enough to make a few drops of water bounce.
- After its first use, it is not necessary to grease the iron unless the batter is very low in fat.
- Handle the batter as little as possible. Overbeating tends to toughen waffles.
- Spoon or pour the batter in the center of the preheated iron. Spread the batter with a wooden spoon to within 1 inch of the edges.
- The waffle will send out a jet of steam at first. When the steaming has dwindled down to a whisper, check to see if the waffle is golden brown. If not, cook it a little longer.
- Subsequent waffles will take less time than the first.
- Waffles can be made with many different kinds of flours, can incorporate fruits, vegetables, nuts, or seeds, and can be served as a base for creamed chicken or tuna, creamed mushrooms, or

as dessert with fruit or carob syrups, whipped cream, or ice cream.

- While you have the iron hot, it's a good idea to make extra waffles and freeze them. On a no-time-to-cook day, pop them in the toaster and you'll have the basis for a good meal in jig time. Or wrap a frozen waffle or pancake in a slightly damp paper towel, microwave on high for 45 to 60 seconds, and serve.

Apple Cinnamon Walnut Pancakes

These pancakes fill the house with a heartwarming fragrance that makes everyone feel very welcome and teases the appetite.

1½ cups apple juice
2 eggs, lightly beaten
2 tablespoons tahini (sesame butter)
1 cup whole wheat pastry flour
½ cup oat bran

2 tablespoons wheat germ
1½ teaspoons baking powder
1 teaspoon grated orange rind
½ teaspoon cinnamon
pinch of nutmeg
½ cup chopped walnuts

In a mixing bowl or food processor, blend together apple juice, eggs, and tahini.

In another bowl, stir together the flour, bran, wheat germ, baking powder, orange rind, cinnamon, and nutmeg. Add to the liquid ingredients with the walnuts and stir just until ingredients are combined. Batter should be lumpy.

Using ¼ cup per pancake, pour batter onto an oiled griddle. When bubbly, turn and brown the other side.

Yield: Makes 12 pancakes.

Each pancake provides: 150 cal, 7 g pro, 3 g unsat fat.

Rhode Island Johnnycakes

You don't have to live in Rhode Island to enjoy these creamy-centered pancakes, which were originally called *journey cakes*, because they provided sustenance for travelers long before the advent of fast foods on the highways.

1 cup yellow cornmeal	*1 cup boiling water*
1 tablespoon honey	*1 egg*
¾ teaspoon vegetable seasoning	*½ cup skim milk*

In a medium bowl, combine cornmeal, honey, and seasoning. Add the boiling water and stir until smooth.

In a small bowl, blend together the egg and milk. Stir into the cornmeal mixture until well blended.

Drop batter by the tablespoon onto hot, buttered skillet or griddle, and cook until well browned on bottom and bubbles appear on top—about 2 to 3 minutes. With a spatula, turn the pancakes and cook until the underside is browned—about 2 minutes.

Yield: Makes about 18 pancakes.

Each pancake provides: 34 cal, 7 g pro, less than 1 g fat.

Zucchini Cheese Pancakes

Serve these savory pancakes with applesauce or tomato sauce and grated Parmesan cheese.

3½ cups shredded zucchini
⅓ cup grated onion
1 clove garlic, minced
⅔ cup grated Parmesan cheese
4 eggs, lightly beaten
½ cup whole wheat pastry
  flour

¼ cup oat bran
¼ cup wheat germ
2 tablespoons lecithin granules
½ teaspoon oregano
½ teaspoon thyme

In a large bowl, combine zucchini, onion, garlic, and cheese. Mix in the eggs, then the flour, oat bran, wheat germ, lecithin, oregano, and thyme.

Using about ¼ cup for each pancake, pour batter onto a hot, buttered skillet or griddle and flatten with a wooden spoon. Cook about 3 minutes or until brown, then turn and brown the other side.
Yield: Makes 32 pancakes.
Each pancake provides: 39 cal, 2.5 g pro, 1 g fat.

Amaranth Yogurt Pancakes
with Strawberry Sauce

High-protein amaranth, "the ancient food of the future," gives these pancakes a new dimension in flavor and nutrition.

PANCAKES

1 cup yogurt
¼ cup water
1 teaspoon baking soda
1 egg
1 tablespoon olive oil

½ cup whole wheat pastry
   flour
½ cup amaranth, barley, or
   rice flour

TOPPING

2 cups fresh or frozen
   strawberries
2 tablespoons honey

2 teaspoons arrowroot or
   cornstarch
¼ cup water

TO MAKE PANCAKES:

In a medium mixing bowl, combine yogurt, water, and baking soda. In a small bowl, beat the egg with the oil and add to the yogurt mixture. Combine the whole wheat and amaranth flours, and stir lightly into the yogurt mixture.

Using about 2 tablespoons for each pancake, spoon batter onto a hot oiled pan or griddle. When browned, turn and brown the flip side.

Yield: Makes 16 pancakes.

Each pancake provides: 42 cal, 2 g pro, 1.2 g fat.

TO MAKE TOPPING:

In a small saucepan, combine strawberries and honey. Stir over low heat until just below boiling. Mix the starch and water together, and stir into the strawberry mixture. Cook over low heat 5 to 7 minutes, or until thickened.

Microwave Topping

In a 4-cup glass measure, combine strawberries and honey. Microcook on high, covered, for 1 minute. Mix the starch and water together, and stir into strawberry mixture. Microcook on high, covered, for another minute.

Yield: Makes about 1½ cups.

Each tablespoon provides: 10 cal, a trace of pro, and no fat.

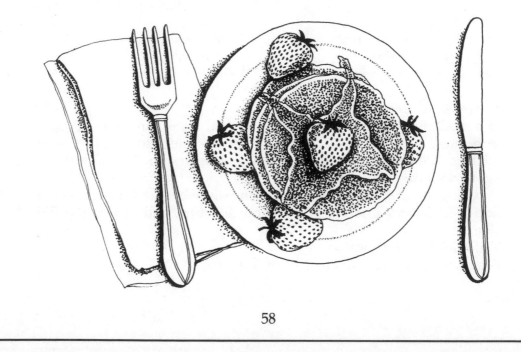

Crunchy Potato Latkes

Potato latkes are associated with the Jewish festival of Hanukkah, the feast of lights. Thankfully we also have the freedom to enjoy potato latkes not just on Hanukkah, but whenever we like, and particularly because nowadays with the advent of the food processor, they are a cinch to make. No more elbow grease, no more scraped knuckles. But, alas, where is that wonderful, hand-grated crunch of yesteryear? Follow this recipe and you can have it all—ease of preparation and that old-time crunch.

4 cups scrubbed, unpeeled potatoes (preferably Idahos), cut into chunks
1 large egg
1 medium onion, cut in chunks
3 tablespoons oat bran
1 tablespoon wheat germ

½ teaspoon (or to taste) kosher salt
¼ teaspoon (or to taste) freshly grated black pepper
dash of cinnamon
2 tablespoons sesame seeds
olive, peanut, or sesame oil for frying

In a food processor fitted with the steel blade, blend ⅔ of the potatoes with the egg, onion, oat bran, wheat germ, and seasonings.

Remove the mixture to a bowl and process the remaining potatoes with the shredder blade. Combine the contents of both bowls.

Heat oil in a heavy skillet. Drop batter by tablespoonful into the hot oil, sprinkle with sesame seeds, then press flat with the back of the spoon. Turn when edges are brown. Place finished latkes on serving platter covered with several layers of paper toweling. Serve sizzling hot, with applesauce or yogurt.

Yield: Makes about 3 dozen latkes.
Each latke provides: 19 cal, 1 g pro, 1 g fat.

Variation 1:
If you'd prefer not to fry the latkes, place them on a cookie sheet, either oiled or spread with nonstick spray, and bake at 350°F until they are well browned.

Variation 2:
Spoon the mixture into muffin tins lined with foil baking cups. Bake at 375°F for 20 to 25 minutes or until well browned.

Variation 3:
Pour batter into oiled 9-inch-square casserole, top with sesame seeds and bake in a 400°F oven for about 30 minutes and you have a lovely potato kugel. Or microwave on full power, covered, for 8 minutes, then brown in a conventional oven at 400°F for 3 to 5 minutes.

Happy thought: You can freeze every one of these variations. When you're ready to serve, put the latkes on a cookie sheet and heat in a 450°F oven for about 5 minutes. Heat kugels and muffins in a 375°F. oven.

Buttermilk Maple Walnut Waffles

You don't have to have a party to enjoy waffles, but waffles do make the breakfast meal a party. For a leisurely weekend breakfast, make them at the table and individualize them—adding fruit, nuts, berries, cheese, tuna, or chicken, according to each one's preference.

*1 cup whole wheat pastry
   flour
2 tablespoons wheat germ
2 tablespoons oat bran
2 teaspoons baking soda
2 tablespoons olive oil or
   butter*

*1½ cups buttermilk or plain
   yogurt
1 egg, beaten
1 tablespoon maple syrup
½ cup coarsely chopped
   walnuts*

In a medium-size bowl, combine the flour, wheat germ, bran, and baking soda.

In a small bowl, blend together the oil or butter, buttermilk or yogurt, egg, and maple syrup. Add to the dry ingredients. Stir in the nuts and mix until ingredients are combined. *Do not beat.*

Heat the waffle iron. Brush lightly with oil or butter. Pour in enough batter to just fill—do not overfill. Close and cook until steaming stops and waffles are crisp. Serve with applesauce or maple-flavored yogurt.

Yield: Makes 6 waffles.

Each waffle provides: 228 cal, 10 g pro, 1 g sat fat, 12 g unsat fat.

Orange Spice Popcorn Waffles

Popcorn flour lightens the texture and lowers the calories of these delicately scented, orange-flavored waffles enriched with wheat germ and oat bran.

2 eggs
1 tablespoon honey
1 tablespoon molasses
¾ cup orange juice
¼ cup skim milk
2 tablespoons oil or butter (melted)
1 tablespoon grated orange rind
¼ teaspoon freshly grated nutmeg

¾ cup whole wheat pastry flour
2 tablespoons wheat germ
2 tablespoons oat bran
½ cup popcorn flour (¾ cup popcorn ground in a food processor, blender, coffee grinder, or seed mill)
2 teaspoons baking powder

In a mixing bowl or food processor, blend together the eggs, honey, molasses, juice, milk, oil or butter, orange rind, and nutmeg.

Sift together the flour, wheat germ, oat bran, popcorn flour, and baking powder.

Stir the dry ingredients into the egg mixture until well blended. Do not overbeat.

Heat waffle iron. Brush with oil or butter. Pour in enough batter to just fill (a scant ½ cup). Close and cook until steaming stops or waffles are baked and light brown.

Yield: Makes 6 waffles.

Each waffle provides: 181 cal, 3.5 g pro, 1.8 g sat fat, 2 g unsat fat.

Oat Bran Waffles

Delicious and good for you too!

1 cup skim milk
¾ cup rolled oats
½ cup oat bran
3 tablespoons olive oil or
　　Healthy Heart Butter,
　　softened (see index)

2 eggs, separated
1 tablespoon honey
¼ cup whole wheat pastry
　　flour
1 teaspoon baking powder
½ cup sunflower seeds

In a small bowl, combine the milk, oats, and bran. Set aside. In another bowl or food processor, blend together the oil or butter, egg yolks, and honey. Add the milk and oats mixture. Blend in the flour mixed with the baking powder. Stir in the seeds.

Beat the egg whites until stiff and fold into the batter.

Heat the waffle iron. Brush with oil or Healthy Heart Butter. Pour in a scant ½ cup of batter. Close and cook until steaming stops or waffles are baked and light brown.

Yield: Makes 6 waffles or 12 portions.

Each portion provides: 124 cal, 6 g pro, 1.4 g sat fat, 6.3 g unsat fat, 2.5 g fiber.

HOT TIPS FOR GREAT CREPES

Crepes are the sophisticated member of the pancake family. The batter is thinner and is usually wrapped around a delectable filling. The filled crepe is generally known as a blintz.

Though they make an elegant presentation, they're as easy as pie to prepare. And unlike the usual restaurant and store-bought variety, made from white flour and oversweetened with sugar, these blintzes are made with a wide choice of whole grain flours and no sugar at all. Only a tiny bit of honey is added to sharpen the flavors.

Use your imagination and the contents of your refrigerator when it comes to filling the crepes. There's no limit to the tantalizing possibilities. Leftovers are perfect fillings. You can dice meat, poultry, fish, vegetables, or fruits to fold in a crepe. One of our favorites is lightly steamed broccoli tucked into a thin slice of mozzarella, then wrapped in a crepe blanket, and lightly sautéed or baked. Or fresh blueberries or blueberry conserves embedded in a cottage or ricotta cheese, wrapped in a tender crepe, and topped with blueberry yogurt.

Crepes can be folded in many different shapes. The most popular shape is the fold-over. Place the best-looking side of the crepe down, spread the filling to within ¼ inch of the edge, then start rolling the crepe into a log shape.

For creamy mixtures, use the pocket shape. Spoon filling into center of the bottom third of the crepe. Roll once, then fold the sides toward the center and roll again. The filling will be nicely enclosed.

The stack or gateau makes a "stand-up-and-cheer" presentation at a brunch. The crepes are stacked with filling between the layers. Lay crepes flat. Spread filling over each crepe, leaving about ¼ inch border, and stack to imposing heights. Sensational when filled with apricot conserves flavored with a bit of rum, the whole thing topped with toasted almonds and puffs of whipped cream. Oo-la-la!

- The crepe itself can be made with varying proportions and various types of flour, a liquid (milk, water, or juice), and eggs.
- Try to make the crepe batter at least an hour before you want to cook the crepes. I like to make the batter the night before. It's easier to cook the batter and it's more tender if it's had a chance to rest.
- The batter should be the consistency of heavy cream. If necessary, thin it with a little water. If it is too thin, add a small amount of flour and let it rest again before using.
- Use an 8-inch pan, which should be heated to medium high. Too hot a pan will burn and ripple the crepe. Too cool a pan produces a tough crepe.
- Heat the skillet until a little water dances when dropped into it. It is not necessary to grease a nonstick pan. For an ordinary pan, rub the surface with butter or oil. Healthy Heart Butter works fine.
- Pour in about ¼ cup of batter, thinly covering the entire surface, then tilt the pan and pour any excess batter back into the container.
- Cook until the top surface appears dry and a peek underneath reveals that the bottom is golden, or until the top peels away from the pan. Bump the crepe out onto a tea towel and fold the towel over it to prevent drying out. Repeat, wiping the skillet with more butter only when necessary. With a nonstick pan, it's not necessary at all.
- To freeze, place crepes, separated by wax paper, between two paper plates. Staple plates together and freeze. To freeze blintzes, place in baking dish or plastic container and freeze.

Apple Blintzes with Raspberry Syrup

These elegant crepes can be made at your leisure and stored in the freezer till the doorbell announces your first guests.

CREPES

3 eggs
1 cup whole wheat pastry
flour

1 cup water
½ teaspoon honey

SYRUP

2 cups fresh or frozen
raspberries
2 tablespoons honey
½ teaspoon vanilla

2 teaspoons arrowroot or
cornstarch
¼ cup water

FILLING

5 tart apples, thinly sliced
2 tablespoons butter
1 tablespoon honey

3 tablespoons raisins
½ teaspoon cinnamon

TO MAKE CREPES:

In a large mixing bowl or food processor, combine eggs, flour, honey, and water and mix to make a smooth batter the consistency of light cream. Pour into a 2-cup measure with a pouring lip and let stand for at least 30 minutes.

TO MAKE SYRUP:

In a small saucepan, combine raspberries, honey, and vanilla. Stir over low heat until just below boiling. Mix starch and water, and add to raspberry mixture. Cook over low heat until thickened, about 5 minutes. This results in a jamlike consistency. Or, if you prefer, the raspberries can be strained through a sieve.

TO MAKE FILLING:
Sauté apple slices in butter until slightly soft. Stir in honey, raisins, and cinnamon. Remove from heat and cover to keep warm.

Pour ¼ cup of the batter into a nonstick 8-inch skillet or crepe pan and tilt to spread evenly. Cook for 1 minute on each side. Remove from pan and place on a towel. Repeat with the remaining batter.

Using about 3 tablespoons, spoon the filling down the center of each crepe, and fold both sides over the filling. Garnish with raspberries or serve with raspberry syrup.

Yield: Makes 16 filled crepes.
Each crepe provides: 83 cal, 2 g pro, 2.8 g fat.
With topping, each crepe provides: 99 cal, 2.2 g pro, 2.8 g fat.

Orange Yogurt Crepes

Enjoy a tangy vitamin C boost with these crepes!

2 eggs
¼ cup orange juice
¼ cup plain yogurt
¼ cup milk
1 cup whole wheat pastry
   flour

1 tablespoon olive oil or
   butter, softened
1 teaspoon grated orange rind

Combine all ingredients in mixing bowl, food processor, or blender and proceed as described in introduction on crepes.
Yield: Makes 16 crepes.
Each crepe provides: 45 cal, 2 g pro, 2 g fat.

Oat 'n' Cheese Blintzes

Oat flour brings a subtle sweetness to crepes, provides as much as 4.5 grams of iron in ¾ cup, as well as lots of oat bran, the soluble fiber that has been shown to lower cholesterol levels.

CREPES
1½ cups oat flour
2 cups skim milk
4 eggs

2 tablespoons oil, butter, or
    Healthy Heart Butter
    (see index for recipe)

FILLING
¾ pound low-fat cottage cheese
2 tablespoons Neufchatel or
    yogurt creamless cheese
    (see index for recipe)
1 egg yolk

1 teaspoon honey
½ teaspoon grated lemon rind
½ teaspoon vanilla extract
⅛ teaspoon cinnamon

TO MAKE CREPES:
Follow procedures as described in previous "Hot Tips for Great Crepes."
Yield: Makes about 20 crepes.
Each crepe provides: 35 cal, 3 g pro, .3 g sat fat, 1.5 g unsat fat, 1 g fiber.

TO MAKE FILLING:
Combine all ingredients. Mix by hand or in food processor.

Place a heaping tablespoonful of the filling onto each crepe. Roll once, then fold the sides over toward the center and roll again. The filling should be nicely enclosed. Place in a lightly buttered baking dish, brush with a tiny bit of butter and bake at 350°F for 15 minutes. The oven does not have to be preheated. The blintzes can also be sautéed. They are tender, wholesome, and delicious.

Yield: Makes enough for 16 fillings.
Each filling provides: 25 cal, 3 g pro, less than 1 g fat.

Variation:
Try this filling for a different texture and taste.

CHICKEN AND CASHEW FILLING

½ cup chopped cashews, toasted	¼ teaspoon freshly ground pepper
2 cups cooked chicken, cut in bite-size pieces	3 tablespoons chicken stock or gravy
1 egg	

Combine all ingredients and proceed as described in introduction on crepes.

Yield: Makes enough to fill 16 crepes.
Each filling provides: 45 cal, 6 g pro, 2 g fat.

Tortillas

From south of the Border, these cornmeal pancakes have won fans all over the country. They're wonderful wrapped around a spicy bean filling. Even children who are non-eaters gobble them up.

*1 cup whole wheat pastry
    flour
4 eggs, beaten
2 tablespoons peanut oil
1½ to 2 cups water*

*1 cup cornmeal, finely ground
½ teaspoon salt or vegetable
    seasoning*

In a mixing bowl or food processor, blend together the eggs, oil, and 1½ cups water.

Combine flour, cornmeal, and salt or vegetable seasoning and blend this mixture with the egg mixture. Add a little more water if necessary to thin to the consistency of light cream. The amount of water needed will vary according to the coarseness of the cornmeal.

Dip a paper towel in a little oil, and wipe the bottom of a cast-iron skillet about 8 to 10 inches in diameter. On medium heat, preheat the skillet. Pour about ¼ cup batter into skillet and tilt or rotate pan, swirling the batter around easily to make a pancake about 6 inches across and ⅛ inch thick. Leave it a few minutes until it is brown on the bottom, then turn it over and leave it a short time to brown the flip side. Don't leave it too long or it may get too stiff to roll or fold.

To keep tortillas warm, stack them, cover with a tea towel, and put them in a warm oven.

Yield: Makes 24 tortillas.

Each tortilla provides: 55 cal, 2.5 g pro, 1.5 g fat.

4

OVEN-FRESH SMART BREADS, BISCUITS, AND BAKED GOODS

Melt-in-Your-Mouth Quick Biscuits
Aunt Betty's Virginia Biscuits
Flaky Crescent Rolls
Breakfast Cake
Wholesome Whole Wheat Challah
Old-Fashioned Cinnamon Buns
Heavenly Brioche
Cinnamon Twist Coffee Cake with Raisins and Nuts
Zucchini Date 'n' Nut Bread

If you have never baked a loaf of bread, you have missed out on one of life's most elemental joys. Nothing gives me more pleasure than watching my family enjoy a loaf of bread that I have magically conjured up, with the help of my oven, a little yeast, flour, eggs, and maybe a little oil.

I love seeing my children share in the same excitement and wonder that I experienced when I watched my mother bake. She would sing as she mixed and kneaded and braided. In my mind there was something magical about the way she filled the house with such a tantalizing, yeasty, appetite-stimulating fragrance, and then produced those beautiful and delicious breads and cakes.

Now that white bread is an everyday empty-calorie commodity, more available than a good, tasty, wholesome whole-grain bread, try using whole wheat flour, or a mixture of whole wheat and unbleached white.

Stone-ground flour is preferable. Keep it in the refrigerator or freezer and buy it from a source where it is kept refrigerated. The regular whole wheat flour which is used in breadmaking is ground from hard winter wheat and contains a high degree of gluten, which helps the dough to rise. When you are baking with yeast, warm the flour to room temperature. Put as much as you need in the oven at 200°F for about 15 minutes or put it in the microwave oven on high for 1 minute.

For quick breads, muffins, cookies, or pies, use whole wheat pastry flour which is ground from soft wheat. It contributes a finer texture.

Both kinds contain the germ and the bran that are removed from white flour and thus provide many life-enhancing nutrients.

If your family is still accustomed to white bread, use only 1 cup of whole wheat flour in your first batch. Gradually replace more of the white with whole wheat. You may never get them to accept a 100 percent whole wheat bread, but don't despair: instead, for every cup of unbleached white flour you use, take away one heaping tablespoon and substitute one heaping tablespoon of wheat germ. Put the wheat germ with some flour in the blender and whiz it fine. This will give the wheat germ a finer texture and will, in effect, sift the flour. Remeasure the flour after blending.

Melt-in-Your-Mouth Quick Biscuits

There's nothing like a basket of crusty biscuits, hot from the oven, round and puffy, lightly browned on top, to fill you with that lovely feeling that Mom's in the kitchen, all's right with the world. Enriched with wheat germ and oat bran, these biscuits provide more than a nostalgic glow. They provide lots of nutrients for sustained energy and fiber for lowering cholesterol.

1½ cups whole wheat pastry flour
2 tablespoons wheat germ
2 tablespoons oat bran
1 tablespoon baking powder

1 teaspoon vegetable seasoning
2 tablespoons poppy seeds
¼ cup reduced-calorie mayonnaise
1 cup skim milk

Preheat oven to 450°F.

In a mixing bowl, sift the flour, wheat germ, oat bran, baking powder, and seasoning. Stir in the poppy seeds, mayonnaise, and milk. Mix to combine ingredients. Batter will be the consistency of thick cream.

Drop the batter by tablespoonfuls onto a large, ungreased cookie sheet.

Bake for 10 minutes or until the biscuits are golden.

Yield: Makes about 20 biscuits.

Each biscuit provides: 52 cal, 2 g pro, 1 g fat.

Aunt Betty's Virginia Biscuits

Even the biscuits have a southern accent at Aunt Betty's. These are especially delicious when spread with unsweetened fruit conserves, but children often prefer them with peanut butter.

1½ cups whole wheat pastry flour	*1 teaspoon vegetable seasoning*
¼ cup oat bran	*⅓ cup Healthy Heart Butter*
2 tablespoons lecithin granules	*(see index for recipe)*
2 tablespoons wheat germ	*2 teaspoons honey*
1 tablespoon baking powder	*⅔ cup buttermilk or yogurt*

Preheat oven to 450°F.

In a mixing bowl, sift together the flour, oat bran, lecithin, baking powder, and seasoning. Remove ½ cup of this flour mixture and set aside.

Add the butter to the remaining flour mixture and blend it in with a pastry blender or 2 knives. Combine the honey and buttermilk, and stir until well blended. Add to the bowl.

Turn the dough out onto a lightly floured surface (use the reserved flour) and gently knead in all the remaining flour. Roll out the dough into a circle ½-inch thick. Using a 2-inch cutter or an inverted glass, cut out as many biscuits as possible. Place them 1 inch apart on a baking sheet, lightly greased or lined with parchment paper.

Bake in the middle of the oven 10 to 12 minutes or until the biscuits are golden brown.

Yield: Makes about 18 biscuits.

Each biscuit provides: 71 cal, 2 g pro, 3 g unsat fat.

Flaky Crescent Rolls

These tender, flaky rolls add a touch of elegance to breakfast and they are melt-in-your-mouth delicious.

2 tablespoons baking yeast	1 cup warm water
1 cup lukewarm water	3 eggs
1 cup vegetable oil or Healthy	6 cups whole wheat flour
Heart Butter (see index	1 teaspoon water
for recipe)	¼ cup sesame seeds
3 tablespoons plus 1 teaspoon	
honey	

Dissolve the yeast in the lukewarm water. Stir in 1 teaspoon honey. Set aside for 5 minutes.

In a large bowl, mix the oil or butter, 3 tablespoons honey, and the warm water.

Beat 2 of the eggs. Add the beaten eggs and the yeast mixture to the oil mixture. Gradually stir in the flour, mixing well, but do not knead. Cover and chill in the refrigerator for about 2 hours.

Lightly oil a baking sheet or line it with parchment paper.

Turn the dough out onto a floured surface. Divide it into 3 parts and roll each part into a large circle as thin as possible.

Make an egg wash by combining the remaining egg with a teaspoon of water and brush evenly over rolled-out dough. Sprinkle with sesame seeds.

Cut each circle into wedges about 2 inches wide at the circumference. Roll each wedge toward the center. Dip the top in the egg wash and then in sesame seeds.

Place on prepared baking sheet and curve each roll slightly into the shape of a crescent. Let rise in warm place for 1½ hours.

Bake in preheated 400°F oven for 25 minutes or until golden. Serve warm. To reheat, wrap in foil and bake at 400°F for 5 minutes. **Yield:** Makes 4 dozen rolls.

Each roll provides: 98 cal, 2.5 g pro, 1 g sat fat, 4 g unsat fat.

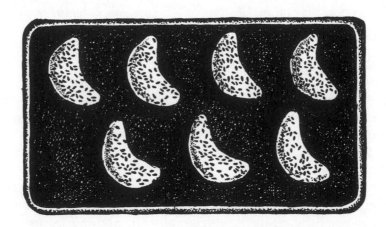

Breakfast Cake

Start this cake first thing Sunday morning and the delicious aroma will get your sleepyheads out of bed quicker than an alarm clock. Serve it with applebutter and yogurt.

¼ cup Healthy Heart Butter (see index for recipe)
½ cup honey or molasses
1 cup skim milk
2 cups whole wheat pastry flour
1½ teaspoons baking powder
¼ cup oat bran
¼ cup wheat germ
2 tablespoons soy flour or rice flour
¼ cup chopped walnuts
1 teaspoon ground cinnamon
1 teaspoon grated orange rind
3 tablespoons granola (see index for recipe)
½ teaspoon cinnamon

In a mixing bowl or food processor, blend together the butter, honey or molasses, and milk.

In another bowl, mix together the flour, baking powder, oat bran, wheat germ, soy flour or rice polish, cinnamon, and orange rind. Add this mixture to the milk and honey mixture, and blend to combine ingredients. Do not overmix.

Spoon batter into a greased 9-inch-square pan. Combine the granola, walnuts, and ½ teaspoon of cinnamon, and sprinkle this mixture over the top. Using a spatula, swirl this mixture through the batter.

Bake at 350°F for 30 to 35 minutes. Serve warm.

Yield: Makes 10 servings.

Each serving provides: 186 cal, 6 g pro, .8 g sat fat, 1.5 g unsat fat.

Wholesome Whole Wheat Challah

A high-protein, highly nutritious Sabbath twist. Two loaves of challah are placed on the Sabbath table to recall the double portion of manna that fell in the desert every Friday. Sliced challah makes wonderful toast to serve under poached eggs for breakfast.

2 tablespoons dry yeast or 2
    yeast cakes
½ cup lukewarm water
4 eggs
3 tablespoons olive or
    vegetable oil
1 tablespoon honey
1 teaspoon salt (optional)
2 cups hot water
4 cups whole wheat bread
    flour
½ cup soy, rice, or oat flour

3½ cups unbleached white or 3
    cups whole wheat
    pastry flour
1 cup unbleached white or
    popcorn flour
(To make popcorn flour, pop
    the corn, blenderize,
    then strain. Popcorn
    flour adds lightness to
    whole wheat flour.)
poppy, sesame, or caraway
    seeds to taste

Dissolve the yeast in ½ cup lukewarm water and set aside. Beat the eggs and reserve 2 tablespoons to be used for brushing the loaves later. In a large bowl, combine oil, honey, salt (if you're using it), eggs, and hot water. When the mixture cools to a bit hotter than lukewarm, add the yeast mixture. Mix well with a wooden spoon. Gradually add the 4 cups of whole wheat bread flour, reserving some for the kneading board. Mix well.

Combine remaining flours and add to the yeast mixture. Work them in. Let the dough rest for 10 minutes. Knead dough on a floured board for about 10 minutes. Add more flour if the dough is too sticky. Oil your hands for smoother handling.

Form the dough into a ball. Place the ball in an oiled bowl, and turn to grease all sides. Cover with a damp tea towel and set in a warm place (on a radiator or the back of the stove) for about 2 hours—until it doubles in bulk.

Punch the dough down and knead it again for a few minutes. Divide the dough in half and shape each half into a braided loaf.

To make a braid, divide each portion into 3 equal parts. Roll each part out a bit longer than the pan in which you plan to bake the challah. Pinch the strands together at one end. Then take the piece on the outer right, cross it over the middle one. Then take the piece on the outer left and also cross it over the middle. Repeat this procedure until you have completed shaping the bread. Pinch the strands together at the other end.

To make the challah extra fancy, divide the dough into 4 equal parts and make a thin braid out of the fourth section. Place this braid down the center of the large braid. This braid bakes up very crisp and is the nosher's crunchy delight.

After shaping the loaves, place both on a greased baking sheet, or in greased bread pans, and let them rise in a warm (not hot) place until double in bulk—for an hour or so.

Preheat oven to 400°F.

Add a teaspoon of water to the reserved egg and brush the surface of both loaves. Sprinkle with poppy, sesame, or caraway seeds.

When the loaves have risen, bake them for 15 minutes. Then reduce the heat to 350°F and continue baking for 45 minutes.

Yield: Makes 2 large loaves. Each loaf makes 20 slices.

Each slice provides: 101 cal, 3 g pro, 1.5 g fat.

Note: Day-old challah makes marvelous French toast.

Variation:

Challah dough is very versatile. Try shaping some of it into small round balls. Let them rise until double in bulk, brush with egg wash, top with sesame seeds, then bake on a greased baking sheet in a preheated 375°F oven for about 20 minutes. Use them as breakfast rolls, for tuna sandwiches, or hamburger buns. Make them long and narrow like hot dog rolls, then spread with peanut butter, fill with half a banana sliced lengthwise, and top with sunflower seeds. Even recalcitrant breakfast-snubbers love these.

Old-Fashioned Cinnamon Buns

The very name of these fragrant, slightly sweet buns brings back memories of the tantalizing aromas in my Auntie Nina's kitchen and of her loving urging to "Eat, eat, you need your strength!" Believe me, nobody needed any urging to eat those warm, cinnamony "pultabulchas."

To make these delicious buns, you can use coffee-cake dough or challah dough. Since you already have challah dough, remove ⅓ of it after the first rising. Make a well in the center and add this mixture:

3 tablespoons softened butter	*½ cup chopped pecans or*
¼ cup honey	*walnuts*
1 teaspoon cinnamon	*1 teaspoon grated orange peel*
½ cup raisins or currants	

80

Combine these ingredients, then knead them into the dough.

Form into small rolls or flatten out egg-size portions, then fold 2 sides towards the center. Brush with egg wash (1 egg yolk beaten with 1 teaspoon cold water) and top with cinnamon and crushed nuts. Preheat oven to 350°F. Let rise again until they double in bulk. Bake for 25 to 35 minutes.

Yield: Makes approximately 12 pultabulchas.

Each pultabulcha provides: 96 cal, 6 g pro, 1.8 g sat fat, 4 g unsat fat.

Heavenly Brioche

These French rolls, first cousins to croissants, contribute a touch of class and a heavenly fragrance to any breakfast. Crunchy on the outside, light as a cloud on the inside, they're a breeze to make. They can be stored for as long as a week in the refrigerator or made part way and refrigerated overnight, or for several days. Then you can have fresh-from-the oven flavor and aroma to grace your breakfast or brunch table without any hassle.

3 to 4 cups unsifted whole wheat bread flour (not pastry flour)
½ teaspoon salt (optional)
1 package or 1 tablespoon active dry yeast
½ cup milk
¼ cup water

¼ cup honey
½ cup Healthy Heart Butter (see index for recipe)
3 eggs (at room temperature)
1 egg yolk
1 egg white, slightly beaten
2 tablespoons sunflower or sesame seeds

If you keep your flour in the freezer, as I do, warm it to room temperature, either by placing it in a conventional oven at 200°F for 10 to 15 minutes or by microwaving, uncovered, for 30 seconds on full power.

In a large mixing bowl, mix together 1 cup of the warmed flour, the salt, if you're using it, and the undissolved yeast.

In a saucepan, combine the milk, water, honey, and butter and heat over low heat until liquids are very warm (120° to 130°F). Butter does not have to melt. Add this mixture gradually to the dry ingredients and beat 2 minutes at medium speed, in electric mixer, scraping bowl occasionally. Add eggs, extra egg yolk, and ¾ cup of flour. Beat at high speed for 2 minutes, scraping bowl occasionally. Stir in enough additional flour to make a stiff batter.

Cover the bowl with plastic wrap or a tea towel, and let rise in a warm place until more than doubled in bulk—about 2 hours.

Stir the batter down and beat for 2 minutes. Cover tightly with plastic wrap and refrigerate for 2 hours or overnight.

Punch dough down and turn out onto a lightly floured board. Set aside about ¼ of the dough. Cut the larger piece into 24 equal pieces. Form each piece into a smooth ball and place in large well-greased muffin tins. Cut the small piece into 24 equal parts. Form into small balls.

With a moistened finger, make a deep indentation in center of each large ball. Press a small ball into each indentation. Cover and let rise in a warm place until doubled in bulk, in about 45 minutes.

Preheat oven to 350°F.

Bake for 25 minutes. Remove from oven and let cool in tins for 25 minutes. Remove from pans and place on wire rack to cool thoroughly. Wrap tightly in plastic bags and refrigerate up to 1 week.

To brown the brioche for your breakfast or brunch, place as many as you need in greased muffin tins. Brush them with slightly beaten egg white. Top with sunflower or sesame seeds and bake at 350°F for 12 minutes or until nicely browned. Remove from muffin tins and cool on wire rack, or serve hot. Any leftover browned brioche can be reheated in the toaster oven.

Yield: Makes 2 dozen.

Each brioche provides: 117 cal, 3.5 g pro, 1 g sat fat, 4 g unsat fat.

Cinnamon Twist Coffee Cake
with Raisins and Nuts

So pretty, you can eat it with your eyes.

3 cups unsifted whole wheat bread flour (not pastry flour)	¼ cup honey
	2 tablespoons butter
	1 egg
½ teaspoon salt (optional)	½ cup raisins
1 package or 1 tablespoon active dry yeast	1 teaspoon melted butter
	½ cup chopped walnuts
½ cup milk	2 to 3 tablespoons honey
⅓ cup water	1 teaspoon cinnamon

Warm the flour to room temperature by placing in conventional oven at 200°F for 15 minutes, or microwave, uncovered, for 30 seconds on full power.

In a large mixing bowl, thoroughly mix 1 cup of the flour, the salt, if you're using it, and the undissolved yeast.

In a saucepan, combine milk, water, honey, and 2 tablespoons of butter. Heat over low heat until liquids are very warm (120 to 130°F). Butter doesn't have to melt. Gradually add to dry ingredients and beat 2 minutes, at medium speed, in electric mixer, scraping bowl occasionally. Add eggs and ½ cup flour. Beat at high speed 2 minutes, scraping bowl occasionally. Stir in raisins. Add enough additional flour to make a stiff dough. Turn out onto lightly floured board; knead until smooth and elastic, about 8 to 10 minutes. Cover with plastic wrap, then a tea towel. Let rest 20 minutes.

Roll the dough into a 12-inch square. Brush lightly with melted butter. Combine walnuts, honey, and cinnamon. Spread one half of this mixture down the center third. Fold second third of dough over the center third. Spread with the remaining walnut mixture. Fold remaining third of dough over the 2 layers. Cut into strips about 1 inch wide. Take hold of each end of each strip and twist lightly in opposite directions (like wringing out a facecloth). Seal ends firmly. Arrange in a greased 9-inch-square pan. Cover loosely with buttered wax paper, then top with plastic wrap.

Refrigerate 2 to 24 hours.

When ready to bake, remove from refrigerator. Uncover dough carefully. Let stand at room temperature for 10 minutes.

Bake in oven preheated to 375°F about 30 minutes. Remove from pan and cool on wire rack.

Yield: Makes 1 scrumptious coffee cake (12 slices).

Each slice provides: 200 cal, 6 g pro, 1.5 g sat fat, 3 g unsat fat.

Zucchini Date 'n' Nut Bread

Zucchini is a good source of vitamin A and potassium, and is incredibly low in calories.

½ cup chopped dates or raisins
2 cups grated unpeeled
   zucchini
3 eggs
⅓ cup olive or vegetable oil,
   or Healthy Heart
   Butter, softened (see
   index for recipe)
⅓ cup honey
1 tablespoon grated orange
   rind
1 teaspoon vanilla

2 cups whole wheat pastry
   flour
½ cup oat bran
½ cup rolled oats
3 tablespoons wheat germ
2 teaspoons baking powder
1 teaspoon baking soda
1 teaspoon cinnamon
½ cup chopped walnuts,
   pecans, or sunflower
   seeds

Preheat oven to 325°F.

Combine the dates and zucchini. Set aside.

In a large mixing bowl or food processor, blend together eggs, oil, honey, orange rind, and vanilla. Add the zucchini mixture.

In another bowl, mix together the flour, bran, oats, wheat germ, baking powder, baking soda, and cinnamon. Blend this mixture with the liquid ingredients. Stir in the chopped nuts.

Line 2 1-pound coffee cans, or any similar-sized cans with parchment paper or spritz them with nostick spray.

Divide the batter between the 2 cans and bake 1¼ hours.

Yield: Makes 2 loaves; each loaf makes 10 slices.

Each slice provides: 152 cal, 5 g pro, 5 g unsat fat.

5

ELEGANT WEEKEND BREAKFASTS

Apricot Pineapple Drink
Gazpacho on the Rocks
Tangy Pecan Yogurt Dip
Avocado Dip
Chilled Strawberry in Melon Bowls
Cauliflower Kugel
Stuffed French Toast
Fantastic Fruity Flan with Custard Sauce
Kasha-Vegetable and Cheese Skillet
Sweet Potato Boats
Cranberry Pears
Festive Figs
Apricot Strudel
Hot Mulled Apple Juice or Cider

Call it breakfast or call it brunch; the idea is to enjoy a lovely, leisurely meal with family and friends. Any Sunday or holiday around 11 in the morning is a good time for a brunch. It's my favorite way to get together.

A brunch is informal, relaxing, and very easy on the hostess. I like to provide lots of different kinds of breads, bagels, muffins, and spreads, a tray of natural cheeses, a dip with lots of fresh vegetables, a hearty main dish, and scrumptious desserts that bring wide-eyed exclamations of delight. There is enough variety in a menu like this to please the serious calorie-counters, the children, the finicky, and the epicures. Practically everything can be made ahead, leaving you free to socialize and enjoy a fireside chat.

For spreads to go with the breads, serve an assortment of attractive dishes of natural peanut butter, tahini, cashew or almond butter, unsweetened applebutter, and yogurt cream cheese or kefir cream cheese, which is deliciously creamy and has a pleasant tang. (See the index for the recipe for yogurt cream cheese. Kefir cheese is available at health food stores.) Serve dips in hollowed-out green and red peppers. Then invite your guests to consume the "dishes."

Your desserts should be spectacular—delightful to behold, heaven to eat—and, like your dips, they should not zap your guests with zillions of calories.

I like to include with the cut-and-serve desserts one large platter attractively arranged with several pick-up confections—those for which you need no utensils. For example, walnut halvah and carob chews make a lovely platter. I also like to serve foods that fill the house with tantalizing aromas, like yeast-risen coffee cake, spicy apple pancakes, puffy omelets, and soufflés.

And even these elegant foods will neither expand your waistline nor endanger your coronary arteries. I have reduced the fat and the calories, and increased the fiber to make every dish *Smart*.

Apricot Pineapple Drink

A delicate but refreshing eye-opener.

1 can (20 ounces)
    unsweetened pineapple
    chunks, drained
1 can (8¾ ounces) unpeeled
    apricot halves, drained,
    or ½ cup dried apricots
    soaked overnight in the
    pineapple juice drained
    from the can of
    pineapple chunks (re-
    serve drained juice)

1 can (6 ounces) frozen limeade
    or orange juice, defrosted
    and undiluted
1½ cups skim milk

Combine pineapple chunks, apricots, limeade or orange juice, and milk in blender or food processor, and whiz until frothy. Add the reserved juice from apricots and whiz again. Serve immediately.
Yield: Makes 10 servings.
Each serving provides: 68 cal, 1.5 g pro, 7 g fat.

Gazpacho on the Rocks

A zingy flavor that wakes up your taste buds and livens up the conversation.

2 24-ounce cans vegetable-
   juice cocktail
1 cup chopped tomato
2 tablespoons each of chopped
   celery, chopped
   cucumber, and lemon or
   lime juice
1 tablespoon each of chopped
   onion or snipped

chives, chopped green and
   red peppers, chopped
   carrot, chopped fresh
   parsley, chopped fresh
   (or 1 teaspoon dried) dill
2 cloves garlic, minced
   hot pepper sauce (to taste)
   lime slices (garnish)

Pour about 1½ cups of the juice into an ice-cube tray and freeze until solid.

In a blender or food processor, purée the tomato, celery, cucumber, lime juice, onion or chives, green and red peppers, carrot, parsley, dill, and garlic with the remaining juice until smooth. Work in batches if necessary.

To serve, distribute the frozen cubes among short glasses. Pour in the juice mixture, garnished with a slice of lime. Let each guest add hot pepper sauce to taste.

Yield: Makes 10 servings.
Each serving provides: 17 cal, 1 g pro.

Tangy Pecan Yogurt Dip

The zippy garlic flavor is enhanced with the pleasant crunch of pecans.

¼ cup pecans or walnuts, chopped
1 clove garlic, mashed
1 tablespoon olive oil

¾ cup yogurt
½ cup diced cucumber
1 teaspoon lemon juice

In a pretty bowl, combine nuts, garlic, and oil. Add the yogurt, cucumber, and lemon juice. Stir to combine. Chill. Serve with crisp vegetables.
Yield: Makes 1¼ cup.
Each tablespoon provides: 19 cal, .5 g pro, 1.2 g fat.

Avocado Dip

Use scooped-out avocado shells for serving dishes. Place avocado seeds in the mixture to keep it green until serving time.

2 tablespoons lemon juice
½ cup tofu
2 tablespoons prepared horseradish
2 tablespoons chopped onion

¼ teaspoon chili powder
½ teaspoon paprika
dash of cayenne pepper
2 ripe avocados, peeled and pitted

In the order listed, place all ingredients in a blender or food processor and whiz until smooth. Chill in a tightly covered dish.

Yield: Makes 2 cups of dip.

Each tablespoon provides: 22 cal, 1 g pro, 1.5 g fat.

Chilled Strawberry in Melon Bowls

A dish like this says love in the most delicious way. Besides being a feast for the eyes and absolutely scrumptious, it will refresh and energize your guests when the thermometer soars—or even as the thermometer drops and summer fantasies struggle to survive!

1 quart fresh strawberries, washed and hulled
1 cup orange juice
1¼ teaspoons instant tapioca
⅛ teaspoon ground allspice
⅛ teaspoon cinnamon
2 tablespoons honey
1 teaspoon grated lemon rind
1 tablespoon lemon juice, or to taste
1 cup buttermilk or yogurt
2 chilled cantaloupes or honeydews

Set aside 8 strawberries. Purée remaining berries in blender or food processor. Pour into a saucepan. Add orange juice.

In a small bowl, mix tapioca with 4 tablespoons of puréed strawberry mixture. Add to saucepan with allspice and cinnamon.

Heat, stirring constantly, until mixture comes to a boil. Cook 1 minute or until thickened. Remove from heat. Pour soup into a large bowl or soup tureen. Add honey, lemon rind, juice, and buttermilk or yogurt, and blend well. Slice reserved berries and fold into soup. Cover and chill at least 8 hours.

Cut melons in half. Scoop out seeds. Turn upside down on paper towels to drain. Fill melons with luscious strawberry soup.
Yield: Makes 4 servings.
Each serving provides: 194 cal, 5 g pro.

Cauliflower Kugel

This sensational dish will lend pizzazz to your table and can be served as is or topped with melting cheese.

1 large head of cauliflower, trimmed and separated into flowerettes	¼ teaspoon nutmeg
	⅓ cup wheat germ or whole wheat flour or oat bran
1 medium-size onion, diced	3 tablespoons olive or
3 eggs	vegetable oil
¼ teaspoon white pepper	sesame seeds for garnish

Preheat oven to 350°F.

In food processor, using metal blade, combine cauliflower, onion, eggs, pepper, and nutmeg. Process until cauliflower is finely chopped. Add the wheat germ, flour, or oat bran and the oil and process briefly. Turn the mixture into a well-greased 9-inch-square baking dish. Top with sesame seeds. Bake in oven for about 1 hour, until golden brown and crisp. Serve with applesauce or yogurt.
Yield: Makes 8 servings.
Each serving provides: 81 cal, 4.5 g pro, 7.8 g fat.

Stuffed French Toast

This crispy French toast with a creamy blintz filling elevates the super to the sublime. Another plus for this festive dish is that it can be made in advance and refrigerated or frozen, then heated to a crisp fragrance for a grand entrance.

1 cup part-skim cottage or
 ricotta cheese (drained)
1 teaspoon vanilla
½ cup chopped walnuts
One-day-old challah (see index
 for recipe)
4 eggs

1 cup skim milk
½ cup sesame seeds
½ teaspoon vanilla
½ teaspoon ground nutmeg
1 cup apricot preserves
 (unsweetened)
½ cup orange juice

In food processor or mixing bowl, beat together the cheese and 1 teaspoon vanilla until fluffy. Stir in nuts and set aside.

Cut challah in 1-inch-thick slices. Cutting horizontally along the top, make a pocket in each slice about 2 inches deep and 3 inches wide. Fill each pocket with 1½ tablespoons of the cheese mixture.

Beat together the eggs, milk, vanilla, and nutmeg. Spread the sesame seeds on another plate. Using tongs, dip the filled challah slices in the egg mixture, then in the sesame seeds, being careful not to squeeze out the filling. If you're making them ahead of time, store them at this point in refrigerator for up to 2 days or in freezer for up to 1 month.

When ready to serve, cook on lightly greased griddle until both sides are golden brown. Place cooked slices on cookie sheet and place in warm oven to keep hot for serving.

In a small saucepan, heat together the preserves and orange juice. To serve, drizzle the apricot mixture over the hot stuffed challah toast or serve the hot sauce separately, in a glass bowl.

Yield: Makes 8 to 10 slices.

Each of 8 slices provides: 278 cal, 15 g pro, 3 g sat fat, 14 g unsat fat.
Each of 10 slices provides: 222 cal, 12 g pro, 2 g sat fat, 12 g unsat fat.

Fantastic Fruity Flan
with Custard Sauce

This one's an ingenious way to transform day-old bread into a heavenly dish, just like the bread pudding that Mama used to make.

3 eggs
3 tablespoons butter, softened
1¾ cups skim milk
¼ cup molasses
1 teaspoon vanilla
1½ teaspoons cinnamon
¼ teaspoon nutmeg
4 cups of cut-up bread
½ cup oat bran

3 tablespoons wheat germ
12 dried apricots, slivered
12 prunes, slivered
½ cup raisins
¼ cup chopped walnuts
2 tablespoons shredded coconut, unsweetened (optional)

Preheat oven to 350°F.

In mixing bowl or food processor, blend together the eggs, butter, milk, molasses, vanilla, cinnamon, and nutmeg.

In a buttered 13 × 9 × 2-inch baking dish, combine the bread, oat bran, wheat germ, apricots, prunes, and raisins. Pour the egg mixture over the bread mixture.

Garnish with walnuts and coconut.

Bake for 45 to 50 minutes. Serve it with whipped cream and fresh raspberries and live it up.

Microwave Method

Follow above instructions. Microcook on high in a covered dish for 8 minutes.

Yield: Makes 10 servings.

Each serving provides: 350 cal, 14 g pro, 3 g sat fat, 16 g unsat fat.

Kasha-Vegetable and Cheese Skillet

No brunch of mine is complete without this hearty casserole. After hugs and greetings, the first thing my friends do is scan the table in search of this gutsy kasha dish that just hits the spot.

2 tablespoons olive oil or
butter or 4 tablespoons
tomato juice
1 large onion, chopped
1 stalk celery, sliced
1 green or red pepper,
chopped
1 cup sliced mushrooms
1 cup uncooked coarse kasha
(buckwheat groats)

2 cups water or vegetable
stock
1 cup cottage cheese
1 cup corn, fresh, canned, or
frozen
4 to 6 thin slices of part-skim
mozzarella cheese
10 cherry tomatoes and parsley
sprigs

In a large ovenproof skillet with a tight-fitting lid, heat the fat or tomato juice and sauté the onion, celery, pepper, and mushrooms for about 3 minutes. Add the kasha and liquid and bring to a boil, then reduce the heat to low.

Cover and cook for 10 minutes. Turn off the heat and mix in the cottage cheese and corn. Place the mozzarella cheese on top and slide the skillet under the broiler, or place in a conventional oven or microwave just until cheese melts. Garnish with cherry tomatoes and sprigs of parsley.

Yield: Makes 8 to 10 servings.

Each of 8 servings provides: 152 cal, 9 g pro, 2 g sat fat, 3 g unsat fat.

Sweet Potato Boats

A lovely, colorful dish that's rich in many of the nutrients that get your day off to a good start.

3 large sweet potatoes baked in their jackets	½ cup walnuts
	½ cup sesame seeds
1 cup cranberries	2 tablespoons honey
¼ cup raisins	½ teaspoon cinnamon

Cut each sweet potato in half, lengthwise. Scoop out the centers into a bowl, leaving a wall about ¼-inch thick.

In a food processor, process the cranberries until chopped fine. Add the raisins, walnuts, sesame seeds, honey, cinnamon, and the reserved sweet potatoes, and process until all ingredients are well combined. Mound this mixture in the sweet potato skins, place the

boats in a baking dish and bake at 350° for 20 minutes. Arrange on serving dish, then cut each boat in half, widthwise.
Yield: Makes 12 servings.
Each serving provides: 147 cal, 3 g pro, 6 g unsat fat.

Cranberry Pears

Pretty as a picture, this dish brings crimson elegance to the buffet table.

8 firm pears
1 tablespoon lime juice
2 cups cranberries
1 cup apple or pear juice

2 tablespoons honey or to taste
½ teaspoon ground cinnamon
⅛ teaspoon ground cloves

Using a melon scoop, core the pears from the bottom. Leave the stems intact. Brush pears with lime juice, and arrange them upright in a shallow baking dish.

In a 2-quart saucepan, combine the cranberries, apple or pear juice, and any remaining lime juice. Cook over medium heat until cranberry skins pop. Stir in honey, cinnamon, and cloves. Pour over the pears. Bake at 350°F for 30 minutes or until pears can be easily pierced with a knife but still hold their shape. Serve warm.
Yield: Makes 8 servings.
Each serving provides: 143 cal, 1 g pro.

Festive Figs

The fig is one of the few fruits that is more alkaline than acid, due to its large content of minerals—iron, blood-building copper, tissue-strengthening manganese, iodine, and fluorine, which is useful in the composition of tooth enamel and stimulates the metabolism of phosphorous.

12 whole figs
¼ cup chopped almonds
½ cup wheat sprouts
 2 tablespoons unsweetened
    shredded coconut

½ cup dry sherry
2 tablespoons sesame seeds

With a sharp knife, make a slit along one side of each fig. Combine the almonds, sprouts, and coconut. Stuff each fig with this mixture. Place the stuffed figs in a bowl and cover with sherry. Let stand for at least 24 hours. Turn occasionally so all figs get well soaked. Drain. Roll lightly in sesame seeds. As a substitute for sherry, you could use cranberry, apple, pineapple, or apricot juice.
Yield: Makes 12 stuffed figs.
Each one provides: 136 cal, 1.5 g pro, .7 g sat fat, 1.4 g unsat fat.

Apricot Strudel

Serving strudel is a measure of the high esteem in which you hold your loved ones or guests. It is usually reserved for great occasions—weddings, engagement parties, bar mitzvahs, and celebrations in honor of outstanding achievements, such as an Emmy, an Oscar, a Nobel Prize, or a new baby. But you don't have to wait for a great occasion. Strudel makes any occasion "great."

Strudel dough can be made with whole wheat pastry flour. It will taste very good but it will not be quite so "stretchy" while being prepared as when made with unbleached white flour. If you use the white, you can compensate for its vitamin and mineral deficiencies by adding wheat germ to the filling, 1 tablespoon for each cup of flour. Sprinkle it on the rolled and stretched dough.

The filling in this recipe calls for a grated orange and a grated lemon. That means you use the whole fruit, skin and pulp—everything except the seeds. Be sure to thoroughly scrub the fruit before grating.

APRICOT FILLING

2 cups dried apricots, soaked in hot water for a few hours or overnight

¼ cup honey

1 whole lemon, grated and pitted

1 whole orange, grated and pitted

NUT MIXTURE

1 cup crushed walnuts

½ teaspoon cinnamon

1 cup raisins, preferably golden and unsulfured

½ cup cake, cookie, or graham cracker crumbs

½ cup wheat germ

1 cup unsweetened shredded coconut

STRUDEL DOUGH

1 egg
¼ cup vegetable oil (preferably olive)
6 tablespoons warm water
2 cups whole wheat pastry flour or unbleached white flour

a little more oil for drizzling over the dough
ground walnuts (optional)

To prepare the filling: Drain the water from the soaked apricots. (It makes a delicious fruit juice.)

In a food processor, blender, or mixing bowl, blend together the apricots, honey, and half the grated lemon and orange. Reserve the other half for use with the nut mixture. (You can substitute any good-quality fruit conserve, preferably unsweetened.)

To make the nut mixture: Combine the walnuts, cinnamon, raisins, crumbs, wheat germ, coconut, and the reserved grated lemon and orange.

To make the dough: In a medium-size bowl, beat the egg, add the oil and water, then the flour. Knead lightly until the dough is soft. Cover and set in a warm place for 1 hour.

Divide the dough in half. Place one half on a floured tablecloth and roll it out. Pull and stretch gently until the dough is so thin you can see through it.

After the dough has been stretched, spread the nut mixture over the entire sheet. Drizzle a little oil over all. Spread ¼ of the fruit mixture in a line across one end of the sheet about 3 inches from the edge. Fold this 3-inch edge over the fruit mixture; raise the tablecloth, and let the dough roll over and over itself to the halfway point. Follow the same procedure with the other side of the sheet. Repeat the procedure with the second piece of dough.

Place the rolls in a pan or on a cookie sheet lined with parchment paper or greased with a little oil. Brush the strudel with a bit of oil and top with the ground nuts, if desired. Let stand for about 15 minutes.

Preheat oven to 350°F.

Slice the strudel diagonally into 1-inch pieces, but do not cut all the way through. Bake for about 45 minutes. When cool, cut all the way through.

Yield: Makes about 20 delicious pieces.

Each piece provides: 220 cal, 5 g pro, 1 g sat fat, 4 g unsat fat.

Hot Mulled Apple Juice or Cider

Nothing climaxes a good party like a hot beverage. Serve this hot cider and your guests will hit the road with a clear head.

1 quart unsweetened apple juice or cider

1 2-inch cinnamon stick
5 whole cloves

Combine ingredients in a non-aluminum saucepan. Place over medium heat and bring to a boil. Reduce heat and simmer for 15 minutes.

Strain mixture and serve hot in mugs. Or place in a punch bowl and let your guests help themselves.

Yield: Makes 6 servings.

Each serving provides: 78 cal, .25 g pro.

Variation: HOT MULLED PINEAPPLE JUICE
Combine 1 can (46 ounces) unsweetened pineapple juice, 1 2-inch piece cinnamon stick, ⅛ teaspoon ground nutmeg, ⅛ teaspoon ground allspice, dash of ground cloves. Then follow above instructions.

6

SMART BREAKFASTS FOR THE SMALL FRY

Funny Face Fluffy Pancakes
Halloween Freak-Out
Bumpy Grilled Cheese Sandwiches
Banana Splits with Carob Fudge Sauce
Goldenrod Eggs with a Happy Face
"Ice-Cream Parlor" Milk Shakes
Creamy Coconut Custard
French Toast with High IQ Granules

Most children are ravenous in the morning and will eat anything that doesn't eat them first. But some, usually those whose taste buds have been compromised by a diet too rich in sugary things, are too fidgety to sit still long enough to eat a proper meal.

Then there are those children, usually underweight, who are non-eaters. They approach each meal with a closed mouth. Preschoolers, particularly, can become problem eaters. First of all, they don't require as much food as they did in infancy, because their growth rate is slower. A parent who doesn't understand this tends to push food on the little tyke. Then the table becomes a battleground for a war of wills. And nobody wins.

Getting children to eat the kinds of food that build strong bodies and good minds is a real challenge, and a very important one. The preschool period not only sets the pattern for future eating habits, it is also critical for the development of the brain.

For example, while a low-cholesterol, low-fat diet may be fine for you, it is not for a toddler. "Fats—saturated, unsaturated, and cholesterol—are required for the proper physical development of the brain," says pediatrician Ralph E. Minear, M.D., author of *The Brain Food Diet for Children* (Bobbs-Merrill, 1983). These fats support the growth of the brain cells believed to be responsible for a person's potential intelligence level.

Foods like eggs, meat, fish, legumes, whole grains, and whole milk are among the foods the young brain requires, says Dr. Minear. For children 4 to 6 years old, he recommends approximately 1600 to 1800 calories daily, with 42 to 50 percent of the total calories derived from fat. Complex carbohydrates should constitute 35 to 45 percent, and protein 8 to 15 percent. Simple carbohydrates, like those found in sugary foods, provide only empty or "hollow" calories and are not recommended.

Knowing *what* to feed your child is important. But you're only halfway there. Getting the stubborn little tyke to eat it takes creative ingenuity, finesse, patience, sneaky cookery, and a sense of humor.

For instance, when our four-year-old granddaughter told me one morning that she wanted white toast instead of whole wheat with her egg, I said, "O.K., so your eyelashes won't curl today." She blinked and said, "Could I please have two pieces of whole wheat toast—one for each eye?"

The recipes that follow for your small fry will not only make their eyelashes curl, they will also help them to run faster, climb higher, and beat Grandma at Trivia.

Funny Face Fluffy Pancakes

Children love to make funny faces on these pancakes using the prune and apricot whip for the hair, an orange or tangerine section for the mouth, and raisins or carob chips for the eyes. For the very little ones, you be the artist. They will love to gobble up your handiwork.

PANCAKES

2 eggs	¼ cup soy flour
1½ cups plain or vanilla yogurt	2 tablespoons wheat germ
3 tablespoons softened Healthy	1 teaspoon baking powder
Heart Butter (see index) or	½ teaspoon baking soda
a combination of butter	½ teaspoon cinnamon or
and olive or peanut oil	grated orange rind
1 cup whole wheat flour	

PRUNE AND APRICOT WHIP

8 pitted prunes	water or fruit juice to cover
8 dried apricots	½ cup plain yogurt

To make pancakes: Combine all ingredients in blender or food processor and process only until ingredients are well combined. Lightly oil a hot griddle or skillet. Pour about ¼ cup of batter for each griddle cake. When they get bubbly, turn them over and do the flip side for about 2 minutes. Serve with Prune and Apricot Whip.
Yield: Makes 10 pancakes.
Each pancake provides: 118 cal, 5 g pro, 1 g sat fat, 2 g unsat fat.

To make whip: Soak the prunes and apricots in just enough water or fruit juice to cover for an hour or overnight. Or combine fruit with

1 tablespoon of liquid in a microwave-safe container and microwave, covered, on high for 1 minute. When the fruit is softened, combine it with the yogurt and whiz in blender or food processor, until the fruit is puréed. If you have any topping left after the children's art work, it makes a lovely dessert, served in stemmed glasses and topped with lightly roasted sunflower seeds.

Yield: Makes 1 cup.

Each tablespoon provides: 22 cal, 1 g pro, .5 g fat.

Halloween Freak-Out

This ghost-on-toast will delight little ones, especially if they help to make it.

2 slices whole grain toast
2 slices part-skim mozzarella
    cheese

4 raisins
12 sunflower seeds
1 cup alfalfa sprouts (optional)

Lightly toast the bread, then put a slice of cheese on top of each. Cut out eyes and a nose in the shape of triangles, and a big smiley mouth. Let the children nibble on the cutouts. Press the sunflower seeds into the cheese for teeth. Place under broiler for about 3 minutes or in microwave oven, on high, uncovered, for about 45 seconds or until cheese melts. Now have the kids use the raisins for the pupils of the eyes, and the alfalfa sprouts for hair and whiskers.

Yield: Makes 2 servings.

Each serving provides: 145 cal, 7 g pro, 2 g sat fat, 1 g unsat fat.

Bumpy Grilled Cheese Sandwiches

When we give children freedom to order their own meal at a restaurant, they invariably opt for grilled cheese, and more often than not, they want it on white bread. With grilled cheese made in the waffle iron, however, they just can't tell what kind of bread they're eating. I use whole wheat bread or whole wheat pita and let them savor every little bump.

If you must use white bread, sprinkle wheat germ on the bread before adding the cheese. To gradually wean the children away from white bread, switch to oatmeal bread, or use one slice white and one slice whole wheat.

2 slices whole wheat bread or 1 whole wheat pita, split

1 or 2 slices part-skim mozzarella cheese
1 slice tomato (optional)

Heat the waffle iron and brush both sides with a little butter. Put the cheese and tomato between 2 slices of bread or in the pita and place in the waffle iron. Close the iron and check in about 2 minutes. Cool a little before serving.

Yield: Makes 1 or 2 servings.
Each serving on 1 slice bread provides: 105 cal, 3 g pro, 2 g fat.

Variation:
For pizza lovers, use tomato sauce instead of tomato, and add a dash of oregano and a whisper of garlic powder.

Banana Splits with Carob Fudge Sauce

Serve children a food that they don't usually get in the morning and they think they're doing something deliciously wicked. Banana splits always elicit wide-eyed wonder and mischievous giggles. I serve them as a reward breakfast. There is always an excuse to celebrate, and children feel so very important when you prepare something special in their honor. While banana splits look and taste like a rich confection, they are really rich in protein, complex carbohydrates, the B vitamins, and many important minerals.

BANANA SPLIT

2 bananas
½ cup granola (see index for recipe) or any good dry cereal
1 cup cottage cheese

¼ cup unsweetened strawberry preserves
¼ cup carob fudge sauce (recipe below)
coconut shreds for garnish

CAROB FUDGE SAUCE

⅓ cup sifted carob powder
⅓ cup water
2 tablespoons honey

2 tablespoons peanut butter
2 tablespoons orange juice

To prepare banana split: Peel and halve the bananas lengthwise. Spread the cut surfaces with granola. Mix the cottage cheese and strawberry preserves together. Place a scoop of the cottage cheese mixture in the center of each banana half. Cover with carob fudge sauce and garnish with coconut.

Yield: Makes 2 servings.

Each serving with 1 tablespoon sauce provides: 261 cal, 10.5 g pro, 14 g unsat fat.

To make sauce: In a small saucepan, combine all ingredients. Mix well and place over low heat. Simmer, stirring constantly, for 3 to 5 minutes, or until mixture thickens. Store the leftover sauce in the refrigerator. It will keep for weeks. Use it to make milk shakes or frosted bananas.

Use hot or cold.

Microwave Method

Combine all ingredients in a microwave-safe bowl. Microcook, covered, on high for 1 minute. Stir to a smooth consistency.

Yield: Makes ⅔ cup of sauce.

Each tablespoon provides: 26 cal, 1.5 g pro, 1.5 g fat.

*Goldenrod Eggs
with a Happy Face*

This is a very special breakfast dish, reserved for birthdays, holidays, or periods of convalescence. My mother would make goldenrod eggs whenever illness jaded our appetites. Who could refuse the strengthening quality in their gold-and-white goodness? And who could refrain from smiling at their funny faces?

2 tablespoons butter	6 slices whole grain toast
2 tablespoons whole wheat pastry flour	1 slice of red pepper
1 cup hot milk	1 piece of carrot, cut into sticks
⅛ teaspoon pepper pinch of salt	8 raisins or 2 black olives cut in halves
4 hard-cooked eggs	alfalfa sprouts

Melt the butter in a saucepan. Remove from heat and stir in the flour. Cook until it bubbles. Add half of the hot milk at once and the rest gradually, and bring to a boil. Stir constantly, until the mixture thickens. Add the seasonings.

Separate the egg whites from the yellows. Chop the egg whites and add to the white sauce.

Place 4 pieces of toast on 4 plates. When making this dish for very young children, cut the toast into bite-size squares. Ladle the egg-white mixture over the toast. Put the egg yolks in a strainer and with a wooden spoon push the yolks through the strainer to make golden hairdos on top of the egg-white mixture. Use a piece of red pepper to make a smiling mouth, a piece of carrot for a Pinocchio-style nose, and raisins or black olives for the eyes. Alfalfa sprouts make lovely eyebrows.

Cut the other 2 pieces of toast in half diagonally and place a 3-cornered hat on each goldenrod head. Serve with a giggle.

Yield: Makes 4 servings.

Each serving provides: 202 cal, 11 g pro, 7 g sat fat, 7 g unsat fat.

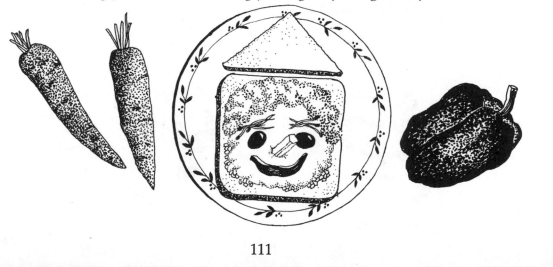

"Ice-Cream Parlor" Milk Shake

There's nothing like this milk shake to intrigue a child who just doesn't want to eat. Line up all the ingredients and let the little one put them in the blender or food processor. They just can't wait to turn the switch, hear the motor, and watch it foam up. Then let them guzzle it through a straw—just like at a real soda fountain.

1 cup milk
2 tablespoons peanut butter
1 mellow banana

1 tablespoon carob powder
1 tablespoon honey, maple
   syrup, or molasses

In blender or food processor, combine all ingredients. Blend for 2 minutes until thick and frothy. If you have any left over, pour into small paper or plastic cups, freeze until mushy, then insert wooden sticks and freeze solid for a health-building popsicle. Pull them out when you hear the siren song of the ice-cream truck.

Yield: Makes 2 servings.

Each serving provides: 201 cal, 8 g pro, 4 g sat fat, 6 g unsat fat.

Creamy Coconut Custard

There are no breakfast-scoffers when this custard is on the menu. It's delicious, nutritious, and a potassium bonanza.

²⁄₃ cup milk
¼ cup unsweetened shredded
    coconut
2 eggs
1 tablespoon molasses

1 cup mashed ripe bananas
¼ teaspoon nutmeg
½ cup granola (see index for
    recipe)

Combine milk and coconut in small saucepan. Simmer over low heat, stirring occasionally, for 2 minutes. Remove from heat.

Preheat oven to 350°F.

In a large bowl, beat eggs; stir in coconut, milk, and remaining ingredients. Turn into greased 1-quart casserole or 4 greased custard cups. Place in pan of hot water. Bake for 30 minutes or until custard is set and top is slightly brown. Top with granola or offer granola on the side. Serve warm, or serve cold with a pitcher of hot milk on the side.

Microwave Method

In a 2-cup glass measure, combine milk and coconut and heat on high, uncovered, for 2 minutes. In another bowl, whisk together the eggs, molasses, bananas, and nutmeg. While whisking, add the hot milk mixture in a thin stream. Divide the mixture among 4 custard cups. Place the cups in a shallow dish. Pour water around them to a depth of 1 inch. Cook on high, uncovered, for 3 to 4 minutes.

Yield: Makes 4 servings.

Each serving provides: 159 cal, 6 g pro, 5 g sat fat, 3 g unsat fat.

French Toast with High IQ Granules

Children, as you well know, go through stages. What do you do when they get to the stage when anything that smacks of health is "gross"? I sailed through this stage by changing the label on the jar I wanted my children to dip into. Usually it was the jar of wheat germ. They were perfectly willing to add "High IQ Granules" to the egg mixture for this crunchy French toast.

2 eggs
⅓ cup milk
⅓ teaspoon cinnamon
1 teaspoon vanilla extract
1 tablespoon dark molasses
2 tablespoons unsalted butter
    or oil

4 tablespoons sesame seeds
3 tablespoons High IQ
    Granules (shhh—wheat
    germ)
6 slices whole grain bread
2 mellow bananas

In a shallow bowl, beat together the eggs, milk, cinnamon, vanilla, and molasses. In another bowl or on a sheet of wax paper, combine the sesame seeds and wheat germ.

In a large skillet, heat the butter or oil or a combination of both.

Dip the bread slices first in the egg mixture, then in the sesame mixture, turning to coat both sides.

Place bread slices in skillet and cook on each side until crispy golden. Slice the bananas over 3 pieces of toast. Cover each piece with another, making a sandwich. Serve with yogurt, maple syrup, or a fruit sauce.

Yield: Makes 6 singles or 3 sandwiches.

Each single provides: 217 cal, 8 g pro, 2 g sat fat, 7 g unsat fat.

Variation:
Use pineapple slices instead of bananas.

7
SMART BREAKFASTS
IN A HURRY
Drinks and Portables

Orange Julius
Peachy Berry Banana Shake
Minty Carob Drink
All-Purpose Dynamite Drink
Sunflower Fruit Smoothy
Pumpkin Granola Bars
Frozen Carob Bananas with Crunchy Granola
Thermos Bottle Cereals
Peanut Butter and Carrot Sandwich

Short on time in the morning? A properly planned rush-hour break-fast is one that can either be partially prepared the night before or that can be made quickly and does not require close attention and split-second timing. This chapter includes sections on blended drinks, precooked hot cereals, and convenient take-alongs to be munched at your leisure. Be sure to see Chapter 1 for cold cereal recipes that are nutritious and quick, too.

TIPS AND TIMESAVERS

- Stock your freezer with single-portion leftovers that can be warmed up in the microwave in less than a minute. Some foods can be prepared in volume for the express purpose of having leftovers for rush-hour breakfasts.
- Make a big pot of oatmeal every weekend. Pack the leftovers in single-portion bowls, cover with plastic wrap, label, and store in the freezer.
- Keep homemade blintzes (see index for recipe), enriched with wheat germ, in the freezer. Heat them in the toaster oven for about 10 minutes or in the microwave for less than 2 minutes. Serve with yogurt or sour cream and unsweetened blueberry conserves.
- Hot whole-grain cereals can be cooked in a double boiler so they don't require constant stirring and won't scorch and stick to the bottom of the pot as they so frequently do when you're in a hurry. Serve them with added oat bran and wheat germ, to boost their protein, vitamin, and fiber content.
- Scrambled eggs are a quick and easy breakfast everyone enjoys. There are 2 ways to get them on the table in a hurry. Prepare the mixture the night before; or the alternative, which is my

favorite way—I assign the job to my husband. He's very proud of his light and fluffy scrambled eggs.

- Set the table the night before. A set table is a silent invitation to sit down and dig in. Make the orange juice the night before or, better yet, cut up a few oranges first thing in the morning.
- If you succumbed to more than 40 winks, or your alarm failed to get you up, and you have no time for a sit-down breakfast or even a rush-hour, stand-up breakfast, then take a portable breakfast with you.

Here are some further suggestions:

- Keep a supply of empty food jars or plastic containers in various sizes. Use them to tote fruit, granola, cottage cheese, yogurt, and beverages.
- Keep a supply of plastic utensils, cups, bowls, and plates, paper or plastic bags, and paper napkins.
- Stock up on single-portion cartons of juice and milk.
- Keep small containers of survival snacks (a mixture of sunflower seeds, almonds, peanuts, and raisins) ready to grab; or hand them to frantic family members as they are rushing for the door.
- Bananas, homemade granola bars, and hard-cooked eggs are portable and sustaining.

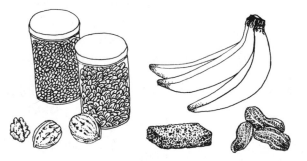

Orange Julius

This delicious drink looks like sunshine and that's how it makes you feel. The vitamin C in the orange juice helps you get more mileage from the iron in the egg and the calcium in the milk.

1 egg*
⅓ cup frozen orange juice
    concentrate

1 cup skim milk
1 teaspoon honey

Combine all ingredients in a blender or food processor and whiz just until the mixture thickens. If it is too thick to drink, eat it with a spoon or dilute it with ice water.

Yield: Makes 2 servings.

Each serving provides: 157 cal, 8 g pro, 1.5 g sat fat, 1.5 g unsat fat.

*When serving children this drink, coddle egg for 30 seconds before using.

Peachy Berry Banana Shake

This is a great way to start the day. Feel free to substitute alternate fruit, depending on what is languishing in your fridge. Use ripe, mellow fruits before they spoil. Dry milk provides more protein and vitamin B_2 (riboflavin). Brewer's yeast zips up the energy potential.

10 strawberries
1 mellow banana
1 peach
½ cup plain yogurt

1 cup apple or orange juice
2 tablespoons dry milk powder
1 tablespoon brewer's yeast
    Strawberry garnish

Combine all ingredients in blender or food processor. Process until smooth and foamy. Pour into 2 tall glasses. Garnish each with a strawberry.

Yield: Makes 2 servings.

Each serving provides: 217 cal, 7 g pro, 1.5 g fat.

Minty Carob Drink

One of my kids called this a chocolate mint you can slurp.

1½ cups skim milk
2 mellow bananas
2 tablespoons carob powder
1 tablespoon honey or
    blackstrap molasses

2 drops natural mint
    flavoring or ½ cup strong
    mint tea

Combine all ingredients in a blender or food processor and whiz until smooth.

Yield: Makes 2 servings.

Each serving provides: 203 cal, 8 g pro, 1 g fat.

All-Purpose Dynamite Drink

Make this convenient, nutrient-rich mix ahead of time and your mornings will be hassle-free. The mix can become the basis for creative blendings of your favorite things.

¼ cup sunflower seeds
¼ cup sesame seeds
¼ cup almonds
¼ cup oat groats or rolled oats
¼ cup carob powder

¼ cup wheat germ
¼ cup oat bran
½ cup nonfat dry milk powder
½ cup soy powder (not flour)

In a blender or food processor, grind the seeds, almonds, and oats very fine. Add the carob powder, wheat germ, oat bran, dry milk, and soy powder, and mix thoroughly. Store in glass jar in the refrigerator or freezer. It can be used directly from the freezer.

To serve, use ¼ cup dry mix to 1 cup of liquid.

Yield: Makes almost 2 cups.

Each ¼ cup provides: 88 cal, 5.5 g pro, 1 g sat fat, 4 g unsat fat.

Variation:

¼ cup All-Purpose Dynamite
    Drink
1 banana, peeled and chunked
1 teaspoon blackstrap
    molasses, honey, or rice
    syrup

¼ teaspoon cinnamon
¼ teaspoon orange rind
1 cup ice water

Combine all ingredients in blender or food processor and whiz until frothy. Serves two lucky guzzlers.

Each drink provides: 115 cal, 3.3 g pro, 2.5 g fat.

Sunflower Fruit Smoothy

This "shake" was concocted by dentist Mike Lerner, of Lexington, Kentucky, who suggests it for youngsters with tooth decay problems. But you don't have to have problems to enjoy its wonderful taste. After all, prevention is better than cure!

½ cup sunflower seeds
2 tablespoons nonfat dry milk
1½ cups unsweetened orange, pineapple, or apple juice

1 mellow banana, peeled and chunked
1 medium-size apple, cut into chunks
1 tablespoon plain yogurt

Grind the seeds in a seed mill or blender. Combine the ground seeds and the remaining ingredients in a blender or food processor and whiz until smooth.

Yield: Makes 2 servings.

Each serving provides: 413 cal, 26 g pro, 18 g fat.

Pumpkin Granola Bars

These crispy, crunchy bars are a convenient and highly nutritious take-along breakfast, or a go-along treat with a milk shake.

¾ cup pumpkin purée, cooked or canned	½ cup chopped peanuts or walnuts, or sunflower seeds
1 egg	
¼ cup Healthy Heart Butter (see index for recipe)	2 tablespoons shredded, unsweetened coconut
¼ cup honey	¼ cup wheat germ
2 tablespoons molasses	½ teaspoon cinnamon
2 cups rolled oats	1 tablespoon grated orange rind

In mixing bowl or food processor, blend together the pumpkin, egg, butter, honey, and molasses.

Add the oats, nuts, coconut, wheat germ, cinnamon, and orange rind, and process until ingredients are well combined.

Spread mixture in lightly greased 15½ × 10½-inch jelly roll pan. Bake in 350°F oven for 40 minutes or until golden brown. While still warm, cut into 3 × 1½-inch bars. For very crisp bars, remove from pan to wire rack and cool completely.

Microwave Method

Spread the batter on a microwave-safe plate or tray and cook, uncovered, on medium, for 8 to 10 minutes, turning the tray 3 times. Watch carefully, as the batter burns easily.

Yield: Makes 30 bars.

Each bar provides: 53 cal, 2 g pro, 1 g sat fat, 2 g unsat fat.

Frozen Carob Bananas
with Crunchy Granola

This is a summer breakfast treat. Keep a supply in the freezer and you're ready for any would-be breakfast skippers.

1 cup carob powder
1 cup water
3 mellow bananas

1 cup granola (see index for recipe)

TO MAKE SYRUP:
In a small saucepan, combine carob and water. Bring to a boil over very low heat, stirring constantly. Cook for about 5 minutes, until syrup is thickened and smooth. Cool. Use to coat bananas. Store unused portion in covered jar in the refrigerator. It will keep for weeks. Makes 1½ cups.

TO ASSEMBLE:
Cut the bananas in thirds. Put the carob syrup in a shallow dish. Put the granola on a sheet of wax paper. Using tongs, roll the bananas in the carob syrup and then in the granola. Place on a tray covered with wax paper and store in freezer. When they are frozen hard, they can be removed from the tray and stored in a plastic bag.
Yield: Makes 9 chunks.
Each chunk provides: 128 cal, 1 g pro, 1 g fat.

Thermos Bottle Cereals

To have your cereal hot and ready as soon as you open your eyes in the morning, take advantage of the thermos bottle. A wide-mouth bottle is preferred, but it is possible to make overnight cereals in the ones with the narrower mouths. Be sure to leave at least 2 inches of ''headroom'' to allow for expansion.

The thermos-bottle method is especially handy for long-cooking grains like whole wheat, barley, steel-cut oats, and millet. They're wonderful for babies who wake up like hungry bears and just can't wait until you get your act together. Start the cereal the night before by putting it in the thermos, where it cooks all night. In the morning, you've got it made.

THERMOS MILLET
>   ¼ *cup millet*
>   2 *tablespoons raisins*
> 1½ *cups water*
> ¼ *teaspoon salt (optional)*

Combine millet, raisins, and water in a saucepan. Bring to a boil, add salt if you're using it, and pour the mixture into a hot, glass-lined thermos. Cork the thermos and lay it on its side to facilitate easy removal of the contents.
Yield: Makes 1 serving.
Each serving provides: 198 cal, 5 g pro.

Peanut Butter and Carrot Sandwich

The combination of peanut butter and whole-grain bread provides a complete, high-quality protein. The linseed oil makes the peanut butter easier to spread and provides valuable linolenic acid.

½ teaspoon linseed oil	1 medium carrot, scrubbed
1 tablespoon peanut butter	and grated
4 slices whole-grain bread	

Combine linseed oil with peanut butter and spread over 1 side of 2 slices of bread. Top with carrot shavings. Close up with the other 2 slices of bread. If you don't have time to finish eating the sandwich, put it in a baggie and take it with you.

For a special treat on those mornings when you do have a few extra minutes, enjoy a grilled sandwich. After you assemble the sandwich, spread a little butter on the top side. Place the sandwich butter side down in a hot skillet for about 3 minutes. Turn and grill the flip side for another 2 minutes.

Yield: Makes 2 sandwiches.

Each sandwich provides: 100 cal, 5 g pro, 3 g unsat fat.

Variation:

Top peanut butter with slices of banana or apple or applesauce and sunflower seeds.

8

BLESS-YOUR-HEART SMART BREAKFASTS

Fruit 'n' Nut Oat Bran Muffins
Hot 'n' Hearty Oat Bran Cereal
Apple Muesli
Sunflower Pancakes with Strawberry Applesauce
Rice Ambrosia with Pineapple
Double Bran Healthy Heart Muffins

The breakfasts in this chapter are targeted for the coronary crowd, but they also provide a big dose of prevention for every one of us. While they are delicious, they are also rich in the nutrients that combat cholesterol and promote the health of the cardiovascular system. These nutrients include:

- Oat bran: While much more study is needed, it is clear that oat bran may substantially bring down cholesterol levels without the side effects of cholesterol-lowering drugs.
- Wheat germ and sunflower seeds: These are high in vitamin E, which may help to maintain normal viscosity in the blood and reduce the risk of life-threatening blood clots.
- Lecithin: Lecithin is a natural emulsifier which some research suggests may increase HDL (high-density lipoproteins), the "good" cholesterol. Lecithin granules can easily be added to beverages, granolas, and other dry cereals. I add them to hot cereals, pancake and waffle batters, biscuits, and muffins. Soybeans and eggs are both good sources of lecithin.
- Magnesium: This mineral is necessary for the proper functioning of the heart and vascular system. A deficiency leads to spasms of the heart muscle, heartbeat irregularities, and angina. It is estimated that 50 percent of the population is deficient in magnesium, probably because it is lost in the refining process. Certain drugs, including diuretics, cause magnesium loss in the urine. Good sources are leafy green vegetables, whole grains, nuts, seeds, and sprouts.
- Copper: In small amounts, this mineral is absolutely essential to proper heart function. Deficiencies in animals lead to fibrosis of the heart and rupture of the aorta due to loss of elasticity. Good sources are nuts, legumes, whole grains, berries, and dried fruits.

- Niacin: This B vitamin, which should be taken under medical supervision, has been shown to reduce platelet aggregation, promote capillary circulation, and lower cholesterol. It can be found in whole grains, sunflower seeds, tuna fish, peanuts, and other nuts.
- Pectin: Research indicates that you're right on target when you make a habit of indulging in the joy of apples, the fruit that is Nature's richest source of pectin. Studies indicate that pectin is an extremely effective cholesterol-lowering agent. Other sources of pectin are oranges, bananas, cherries, grapes, pineapples, tomatoes, peaches, raspberries, and quince.
- Vitamin B_6: This helps prevent damage to artery walls and is a natural diuretic. It is found in whole grains, fruits, and nuts.
- Vitamin C: Since minerals are so vital to heart health, it is important to include in every breakfast some form of vitamin C, which increases the absorption of iron, sometimes as much as 300 percent, and enhances the utilization of many other minerals. Have some grapefruit, an orange, a glass of unstrained orange juice, or a vitamin C supplement.

Fruit 'n' Nut Oat Bran Muffins

These muffins are rich in heart-healthy nutrients. They are loaded with fiber. Four of these muffins provide ½ cup of oat bran and a mouthful of enjoyment in every bite.

½ cup wheat bran
1 cup plain yogurt or
    buttermilk
2 egg whites
2 tablespoons olive oil
2 tablespoons honey, barley
    malt, or rice syrup
1½ cups oat bran
¼ cup lecithin granules
    (optional)
2 teaspoons baking powder

½ teaspoon baking soda
1 teaspoon cinnamon
1 tablespoon grated orange
    rind
¼ teaspoon nutmeg
¼ teaspoon ground cloves
¼ teaspoon ginger
¼ cup chopped prunes
½ cup raisins or currants
2 tablespoons sunflower seeds
¼ cup chopped walnuts

Preheat oven to 400°F.

In a small bowl, combine the wheat bran and yogurt or buttermilk. Set aside.

In mixing bowl or food processor, blend together the egg whites, oil, and honey. Add the wheat bran mixture.

In another bowl, mix together the oat bran, lecithin granules, baking powder, baking soda, and the spices.

Add the oat bran mixture to the contents of the other mixing bowl or processor and mix to combine ingredients. Do not overmix. Stir in the dried fruit, seeds, and nuts.

Line the cups of a 12-muffin pan with paper or foil liners. Spoon batter into the cups and bake for 15 to 20 minutes, or until a cake tester comes out clean.

Yield: Makes 12 muffins.

Each muffin provides: 117 cal, 2.4 g pro, .6 g sat fat, 6.5 g unsat fat.

Hot 'n' Hearty Oat Bran Cereal

On a cold morning, this brisk breakfast will warm the cockles of your heart and delight your taste buds. Bananas bring mellow flavor and a nice jolt of potassium, a mineral that keeps your heart in sync. Pecans provide crunch and elegance, iron, calcium, phosphorous, and vitamins A, B, and C. They are high in polyunsaturated fats and high in calories. Go easy on the pecans if you're weight-watching.

2 cups water	*6 pecan halves, lightly*
⅔ cup oat bran	*roasted**
½ teaspoon cinnamon	*1 banana, sliced*
1 teaspoon grated orange rind	

In a saucepan, combine the water and the oat bran and mix well. Add the cinnamon and orange rind. Bring to a boil, then reduce heat and cook for about 1 minute. Ladle into 2 bowls. Top each bowl with half the banana and 3 pecan halves.

*To roast pecans, place in conventional oven or toaster oven for about 6 minutes at 300°F or in microwave oven on high for about 30 seconds.

Microwave Method

In a 1½-quart bowl, combine water, oat bran, cinnamon, and orange rind. Microwave on high for about 4 minutes or until cereal begins to thicken. Stir well before serving. Ladle into 2 bowls and top with bananas and pecans.

Yield: Makes 2 servings.

Each serving provides: 215 cal, 7.5 g pro, 2 g sat fat, 8 g unsat fat.

Apple Muesli

Muesli is the uncooked grain-and-fruit cereal which helps restore well-being to the patients of the famed Bircher-Benner Clinic of Switzerland. It has been found that certain raw foods contain enzymes that contribute to increased vitality and enhancement of your immune powers.

½ cup pure water	2 tablespoons wheat germ
4 tablespoons rolled oats	2 tablespoons raisins
juice of half a lemon	1 tablespoon honey
½ cup plain yogurt	2 tablespoons chopped walnuts
2 apples, grated, unpeeled	2 tablespoons sunflower seeds

Soak the oats in water overnight. In the morning, add the lemon juice and yogurt. Mix well. Add the grated apples, wheat germ, raisins, honey, chopped nuts, and seeds. Mix it all up and enjoy immediately.

Yield: Makes 2 servings.

Each serving provides: 294 cal, 11 g pro, 10 g unsat fat.

Sunflower Pancakes
with Strawberry Applesauce

It's nice to know that even if you're on a Spartan diet, you can indulge your passion for pancakes in good conscience. The trick is to trade in the overly sweet syrups that are usually associated with pancakes for delicious toppings that lower cholesterol and enhance your heart's potential.

PANCAKES

1½ cups skim milk
2 egg whites
2 tablespoons olive oil
2 tablespoons honey, molasses, rice syrup, or barley malt
1½ cups whole wheat pastry flour
2 teaspoons baking powder
¼ cup wheat germ

¼ cup oat bran
1 tablespoon grated orange rind
2 tablespoons lecithin granules (optional)
3 tablespoons sunflower seeds
1 large apple, unpeeled, washed and cut into dice
1 teaspoon cinnamon

TOPPING

1 large apple with peel, well scrubbed and diced
1 cup fresh strawberries, hulled and cut (frozen berries may be used)

½ cup fruit juice
1 teaspoon grated orange rind
1 tablespoon honey

To make pancakes: In a large mixing bowl or food processor, blend together the milk, egg whites, oil, and sweetener.

In another bowl, mix together the flour, baking powder, wheat germ, oat bran, orange rind, lecithin granules, and sunflower seeds. Combine the 2 mixtures gently. Do not overmix.

Dust the apples with the cinnamon and fold into the batter.

Pour batter onto a hot oiled griddle over moderate heat and cook on both sides until golden brown. Serve with strawberry applesauce.
Yield: Makes 16 to 18 pancakes.
Each of 16 pancakes provides: 94 cal, 4.4 g pro, 2 g fat.

To make sauce: Combine apple and strawberries with juice in saucepan and cook over low heat until soft. Put through the processor. Serve on the side or over pancakes.
Yield: Makes 1½ cups or 12 servings.
Each serving provides: 17 cal, .1 g pro, no fat.

Rice Ambrosia with Pineapple

This lovely dish will delight your taste buds and do your heart good. Brown rice provides fiber, magnesium, and lots of the B vitamins. Pineapple provides vitamins C and A and potassium, but is particularly valuable for its bromelain and copper. Copper is an important micronutrient that has been refined out of the standard American diet, but is necessary for the utilization of iron and for the rhythmic electrical activity of the heart muscle.

1 can (20 ounces) unsweetened crushed pineapple
2 cups cooked brown rice
2 oranges, peeled, sectioned, and pitted or 1 can of mandarin oranges
½ cup coarsely chopped walnuts
¼ cup oat bran
1 pound seedless grapes or a combination of seasonal fruits, diced
1 banana, sliced
1 cup plain, non-fat yogurt
½ cup oat bran crunch for garnish (available at health food stores)

Drain the pineapple and reserve the juice.

In a large glass bowl, combine the rice and the reserved pineapple juice. Add the oranges, nuts, oat bran, grapes, banana, and ½ cup of the yogurt.

Spread the remaining ½ cup of yogurt over the top and garnish with a sprinkling of oat bran crunch.

Yield: Makes 8 servings.

Each serving provides: 180 cal, 5.5 g pro, 3.5 g unsat fat.

Double Bran Healthy Heart Muffins

These muffins are three-way cholesterol fighters. The combination of rice bran, oat bran, and lecithin makes a great team for attacking cholesterol on all fronts. These muffins are also high in protein and the vitamin Bs.

1 cup yogurt or buttermilk	2 tablespoons lecithin granules
2 eggs	1 teaspoon baking soda
¼ cup Healthy Heart Butter (see index for recipe)	1 teaspoon baking powder
¼ cup molasses	1 teaspoon cinnamon
¾ cup applesauce	¼ teaspoon ginger
1 cup rice bran	¼ teaspoon nutmeg
½ cup whole wheat pastry flour	1 tablespoon grated orange rind
¼ cup oat bran	½ cup raisins
	½ cup sunflower seeds

Preheat oven to 375°F.

In mixing bowl or food processor, blend together the yogurt or buttermilk, eggs, butter, molasses, and applesauce. In another bowl, combine the remaining ingredients, except the raisins and sunflower seeds. Add the dry ingredients to the mixing bowl and mix to combine all ingredients. Stir in the raisins and seeds.

Grease 18 muffin cups or line with paper baking cups. Spoon batter into muffin cups to ½ to ¾ full. Bake for 25 to 30 minutes.
Yield: Makes 18 muffins.

Each muffin provides: 116 cal, 4 g pro, 2.4 g sat fat, 2.5 g unsat fat, 4 g fiber.

9
DINNER FOR BREAKFAST

Ambrosia Soup
Cream of Chestnut Soup
Squash and Tahini Soup
Cream of Broccoli Soup
High-Mineral Vegetable Broth
Apple Vichyssoise
Powerhouse Tuna Melt
Baked Potato Pizza
Beanburgers

There comes a time in our lives when we get the breakfast blahs. We tire of the sameness of the menu that greets us every morning. Some of us go so far as to join the ranks of the breakfast skippers. I have a better solution.

It has been said by someone much wiser than I that variety is the spice of life. Our body doesn't mind if our morning source of fiber, carbohydrates, and protein comes from chicken salad on whole wheat bread or from a bowl of hot cereal. Sandwiches, salads, pizza, or lasagna can all be enjoyed for breakfast.

For another alternative, why not try soup? It's comforting, filling, nutritious and cozies up to your innards like a warm blanket. Soup can provide protein, complex carbohydrates, vitamins, minerals, and fiber. It can make you feel full and satisfied on very few calories.

In the summer, potassium-rich chilled soups can be hot weather health insurance. Swimming, tennis, and gardening can all lead to a loss of potassium through perspiration alone. According to researchers at Tulane University (*American Heart Journal*, February 1976), soup is the ideal replacement fluid. Because vegetables, grains, nuts, fish, and meats release their goodness into the fluid in which they are steeped, soup contains "everything one finds in plant and animal tissues."

Far be it from me, however, to suggest that you get up at dawn to brew a hearty breakfast broth. What I do suggest is that when you make soup for dinner, make a little extra. Ladle it into single-portion bowls, and enjoy a bowl of soup for breakfast whenever you wish.

Ambrosia Soup

Sweet potatoes (or pumpkin or squash as a substitute) are wonderful sources of the anti-oxidant beta carotene, vitamin A, vitamin C, the B vitamins, and choline, a substance some researchers think may preserve the brain's ability to reason and remember. Sweet potatoes also provide potassium, calcium, and magnesium.

6 dried apricots
1 cup orange or apple juice
3 cups sweet potatoes,
    scrubbed, unpeeled, and
    cut into chunks
1 cup sliced leeks or onions
1 cup carrots, scrubbed,
    unpeeled, cut into
    chunks
2 large stalks celery,
    including tops, sliced
1 large or 2 small shallots,
    chopped

1 mellow banana
1 tablespoon grated orange
    rind
½ teaspoon cinnamon
    grating of nutmeg
    freshly ground pepper to
    taste (optional)
1 cup milk or light cream
2 tablespoons oat bran
    toasted, chopped almonds
    for garnish

Soak the apricots in the fruit juice for 2 hours or overnight. (Or place them in a 2-cup glass measure with 2 tablespoons of juice. Cover with plastic wrap and microcook, on high, for 2 minutes. Do not drain.)

Place the sweet potatoes, leeks or onions, carrots, celery, and shallots in a steamer basket (do not allow vegetables to touch the water) and steam until soft.

Transfer the steamed vegetables to a food processor, fitted with the steel blade. Add the apricots with the juice, the banana, grated orange rind, cinnamon, nutmeg, pepper, milk or light cream, and oat bran. Process until smooth. Check seasoning. Pour into bowls and garnish with toasted almonds.

Microwave Method

Instead of steaming the vegetables, place them in a 9-inch glass pie plate. Cover tightly with microwave plastic wrap and microcook for 6 minutes. Then proceed as above.

Yield: Makes 6 servings.

Each serving provides: 200 cal, 6 g pro, 2 g fat.

Cream of Chestnut Soup

Every time I sip this soup, an exquisite pleasure invades my senses. So flavorful, it works miracles on the morning grumps. Chestnuts have all the rich, hearty flavor of the nut family minus the high-fat content.

*1 pound chestnuts (in the
   shell)
2 tablespoons olive oil
1 medium onion, diced
1 medium carrot*

*2 cups vegetable or chicken
   stock
1 teaspoon honey
¾ cup light cream or
   evaporated skim milk*

With a sharp knife, cut an "X" in the flat side of each chestnut. Cover with water and boil 15 minutes, then peel as soon as they are cool enough to handle.

Heat the oil and sauté the onion for about 2 minutes or until lightly browned. Scrub the carrot and cut into ½-inch slices. Combine the onion, carrot, and chestnuts with the stock and bring to a boil. Reduce heat and simmer until chesnuts are soft, in about 15 minutes. Pour liquid through a colander and reserve it. Purée the chestnut mixture in the food processor. Return to the liquid and reheat. Combine the honey and the cream or milk and add to the chestnut mixture. Heat but do not boil. This soup can also be served at room temperature or chilled. Delicious at any temperature.

Microwave Method

Cut chestnut shells as above. Combine with ½ cup water in a shallow dish, uncovered, and microwave on high for 8 minutes. Peel when they are cool enough to handle.

In a 2½-quart soufflé dish, microcook the onion in the olive oil, uncovered, for 2 minutes. Add the carrot, sliced thin, and microcook, covered, for 3 minutes. Add the broth and the peeled chestnuts and microcook, covered, for 6 minutes.

Transfer the mixture to the food processor and whiz till smooth. Return to soufflé dish, add the cream or milk, combined with the honey, and microcook, covered, for about 2 minutes to reheat.

Yield: Makes 6 servings.

Each serving provides: 200 cal, 4 g pro, .6 g sat fat, 7 g unsat fat.

Squash and Tahini Soup

You've got to taste this soup to believe its smooth, rich, delicate flavor. It's love at first sip. In fact, tahini, which is made from sesame seeds, is one of the ingredients used by Egyptian women in ancient times to enhance their love life. Sesame seeds are 45 percent protein and very rich in polyunsaturated and monounsaturated fatty acids, which lower the level of cholesterol in your blood. I'm not vouching for what they'll do to your love life, but watch out!

1 tablespoon olive oil
2 tablespoons finely chopped onion
2 cups cooked squash or pumpkin
2½ cups stock or water

2½ cups milk
⅛ teaspoon ground cloves
½ teaspoon honey
1 teaspoon lemon juice
2 tablespoons tahini
pumpkin seeds for garnish

In a heavy saucepan, heat the oil, add the onion and cook for only 2 minutes, stirring, until onion is transparent. Add the squash, stock, milk, and seasonings. Stir thoroughly. Bring to a boil, then reduce heat and cook, stirring occasionally, for 15 minutes. Stir in the tahini. Purée the soup in the food processor, then return to saucepan to be heated through. Do not let it come to a boil. Serve hot and garnished with pumpkin seeds. This soup is also excellent when served chilled with a dollop of yogurt or, if you want to be fancy, whipped cream.

Microwave Method (all procedures on high)

In a 2½-quart soufflé dish, microcook the oil and onion, uncovered, for 1 minute or until onion is transparent. Add the squash and microcook, covered, for 2 minutes. Purée the squash mixture in the food processor. Return to the soufflé dish and add the stock, milk, cloves, honey, lemon juice, and tahini. Cover and microwave for 4 minutes.

Yield: Makes 6 to 8 servings.

Each of 6 servings provides: 87 cal, 4 g pro, 2 g fat.
Each of 8 servings provides: 65 cal, 3 g pro, 1 g fat.

Cream of Broccoli Soup

A rich and creamy, very nutritious soup. Broccoli is a member of the cruciferous family, which has been shown to protect against the development of malignancies. It is very high in beta carotene and has more vitamin C than oranges.

1 *large head broccoli*	¼ *cup whole wheat flour*
2 *tablespoons minced onion*	4 *cups water or vegetable*
2 *celery stalks, sliced*	*broth*
2 *tablespoons butter or*	2 *cups milk or light cream or*
Healthy Heart Butter (see	*half of each*
index for recipe)	*dash of nutmeg*

Wash broccoli and steam it or cook in a small amount of boiling water just until crispy tender. Whiz in blender or food processor until puréed.

Sauté onion and celery in the butter. Blend in the flour, then stir in the water or broth.

Cook, stirring, until slightly thickened. Stir in broccoli, cream or milk, and nutmeg.

Microwave Method (all procedures on high)
In a 2½-quart soufflé dish, microcook the onion, celery, and but-

ter, uncovered, for 1½ minutes or until onion is softened but not brown. Stir in the broccoli. Microcook, covered, for 2 to 3 minutes or until broccoli is tender. Substitute 2 tablespoons of cornstarch for the whole wheat flour, and stir it in. Add the water or broth and mix well. Microcook, uncovered, for 3 to 4 minutes or until the mixture is thickened and bubbly, stirring twice. Combine the hot broccoli mixture and cream or milk in the food processor and process till the mixture is nearly smooth. Pour back into the soufflé dish and microcook, uncovered, for 1 minute or till the mixture is heated through. Do not boil. Garnish with grated nutmeg.

Yield: Makes 6 servings.

Each serving provides: 119 cal, 5 g pro, 5 g fat.

High-Mineral Vegetable Broth

This broth adapted from a Gaylord Hauser recipe is a favorite at many health spas.

1 cup shredded carrots
1 tablespoon chopped parsley
1 tablespoon chopped chives
1 quart water (use vegetable
    cooking water or water
    from soaking seeds for
    sprouting)

1 cup tomato juice or 1 cup
    chopped tomatoes
1 teaspoon vegetable seasoning
1 teaspoon honey
1 tablespoon nutritional yeast
    (optional)

In a large soup pot, combine the carrots, parsley, chives, and water. Cover and cook slowly for 30 minutes. Add tomato juice (or tomatoes), vegetable seasoning, honey, and yeast, if desired. Let it cook 5 or more minutes. If you want a clear broth, strain and serve. I like to purée the whole thing in the food processor. This makes a thicker, but very hearty broth and will provide fiber as well as a gold mine of nutrients.

Microwave Method (all procedures on high)
    In a 2½-quart soufflé dish, combine carrots, parsley, chives, and water. Cover and microcook for 5 minutes. Add the tomato juice, vegetable seasoning, and honey, and microcook, covered, for 1 minute and 30 seconds. Strain or purée in a food processor.
Yield: Makes 4 servings.
Each serving provides: 30 cal, 2 g pro.

Apple Vichyssoise

This soup has a smooth-as-velvet elegance.

1 tablespoon butter
¾ cup finely chopped leeks,
    white part only, or
    onions
2 large, tart apples, coarsely
    chopped
¼ teaspoon curry powder

2 medium-size potatoes, diced
3 cups vegetable stock or
    water
1½ cups buttermilk or yogurt
2 tablespoons finely chopped
    celery leaves (garnish)

In a 3-quart soup pot, melt the butter. Add the leeks or onion, and sauté on low heat until limp. Stir in the apples, curry powder, and potatoes. Cook 5 minutes longer over medium heat. Add the stock or water, bring to a boil, then lower heat and cover the pot. Simmer for 20 minutes or until potatoes are fork-tender. Cool slightly.

In a blender or food processor, purée soup in small batches until smooth. Return to pan or large bowl and stir in the buttermilk or yogurt. Cover and chill until serving time.

Before serving, stir soup well and garnish with celery leaves.
Yield: Makes 4 servings.
Each serving provides: 150 cal, 5.5 g pro, 3.5 g fat.

Powerhouse Tuna Melt

I plan a breakfast like this for my family on days when they have a full schedule of activities with little time for real meals. Tuna is highest of all fish in protein, as much as 45 grams in a 6½-ounce can. Peanuts are an excellent source of pantothenic acid, the B vitamin that helps you to cope with stress. They are also a good source of niacin, a nutrient associated with good mental health and good skin.

1 can (6½ ounces) water-packed tuna, drained and flaked
2 hard-cooked eggs, chopped
⅓ cup chopped peanuts
2 tablespoons reduced-calorie mayonnaise
2 tablespoons plain yogurt
1 teaspoon prepared mustard
3 English muffins, split and toasted
¼ cup wheat germ (optional—see below)
6 slices part-skim mozzarella cheese

Combine, tuna, eggs, and peanuts in a bowl. In a separate small bowl, mix together the mayonnaise, yogurt, and mustard. Add this mixture to the tuna and blend well.

If the English Muffins are not whole wheat, sprinkle some wheat germ over each, then spread the tuna mixture over the wheat germ, and top each with a slice of cheese.

Place in toaster oven or microwave until cheese melts.

Variation:
Can also be made on whole wheat or rye bread.
Note: Make as many of these as you need and reserve the remaining tuna salad for a lunch to go.

Yield: Serves 6 hearty eaters.
Each serving provides: 273 cal, 23 g pro, 5 g sat fat, 7 g unsat fat.

Baked Potato Pizza

There's nutritional gold in baked potatoes—potassium, magnesium, some calcium, traces of the B vitamins, and almost as much vitamin C as you get in half a grapefruit. They also provide fiber and those good complex carbohydrates that keep your body's motor running in high gear. All this and only 145 calories in a good-size spud. The pizza topping provides more go-power and lots of pizzazz.

2 good-size baked potatoes
½ cup tomato or spaghetti sauce

¼ teaspoon oregano
2 tablespoons grated part-skim mozzarella cheese

Cut the potatoes in halves the long way. Top each with 2 tablespoons of tomato sauce, a bit of oregano, and a tablespoon of cheese. Broil in a toaster oven until cheese is melted.

Microwave Method

Assemble the potatoes as above and microcook on high, uncovered, for 2 minutes.
Yield: Makes 2 to 4 servings.
Each half potato portion provides: 93 cal, 4 g pro, 1.5 g sat fat, 1 g unsat fat.

Beanburgers

This is a very tasty high-fiber burger that is often preferable to its counterpart in the beef family, especially for breakfast. The combination of beans, sunflower seeds, and wheat germ makes it a complete protein. The cheese, if you use it, increases the protein value even more and contributes calcium, flavor, and stick-to-your-ribs satiety. These beanburgers can be made ahead of time and heated in the microwave or toaster oven in the morning.

2 cups cooked beans (1 cup raw), preferably red (kidney) or pink (fava) variety
½ cup sunflower seeds
¼ cup chopped onion
½ teaspoon chili powder
2 tablespoons olive oil
3 to 4 tablespoons tomato sauce or catsup
¼ cup wheat germ
¼ cup oat bran
8 thin slices low fat mozzarella or cheddar cheese (optional)

In a food processor using the steel blade, blend together the beans, seeds, onion, and chili powder until smooth. Add the oil, tomato sauce or catsup, wheat germ, and oat bran. Process until ingredients are well combined.

Form into 8 small patties. Place on lightly oiled baking sheet and bake at 350°F for 15 to 20 minutes or until lightly browned and crusty. **Yield:** Makes 8 small burgers: 4 servings.

Each burger without cheese provides: 125 cal, 8 g pro, 2 g sat fat, 4.6 g unsat fat.

10

LEAN, HI-ENERGY BREAKFASTS FOR DIETERS

Cheesy Banana Toast
Skinny Kiwi Parfait
Reduced-Calorie Granola
Hot Apple Oat Bran Crunch
Slenderizing Fruit Cocktail
Skinny Wheat Crepes

When you skip breakfast in order to save calories, you are sabotaging your weight-loss program. You not only accentuate your hunger, thus inviting unwise snack attacks, you also suffer significant loss of stamina and efficiency, making it burdensome to pursue a regular exercise program, which is your best ally in the weight-loss game.

If you are limiting your calorie intake, plan to consume more of those calories in the morning, when your metabolism is in high gear and can more efficiently use up those calories in the production of energy.

Learn how to eat smartly for good health and vitality. Rather than count calories, learn to count nutrients. Never eat an empty calorie and you will no longer yo-yo from fat to skinny to fat again. You will no longer need wardrobes in two sizes. Your taste buds will be sharpened and you will enjoy every bite of nutrient-rich food you put in your mouth. Best of all, you will lose weight and feel great.

While most of the recipes in this book can be enjoyed by dieters, those in this chapter are a little more stringent in the calorie department. And while providing energizing nutrients, they are low in fat. However, don't go overboard and eliminate all fats from your diet. According to pathologist Roy L. Walford, M.D., of the School of Medicine, University of California at Los Angeles, fats can be safely limited to 8 percent of our daily calories (see *The 120-Year Diet*, Simon & Schuster, 1986).

Enjoy these recipes, take a nice walk every day, don't eat what the kids leave on their plates, go to bed before you get snack-happy, and watch the scales do a nosedive.

Cheesy Banana Toast

This little treat is delicious, satisfying, and easy to prepare. The cheese provides ample protein for stamina, the whole-grain bread provides complex carbohydrates for energy and B vitamins that help you to cope, and the banana provides potassium and B_6, which is a natural diuretic.

2 slices whole-grain bread
½ cup low fat cottage cheese
    dash of cinnamon

1 banana, sliced
1 tablespoon sesame seeds

Spread each piece of bread with the cheese. Sprinkle with cinnamon and arrange banana slices over top. Place on toaster oven pan and toast until cheese is hot and bread is slightly toasted.
Yield: Makes 1 or 2 servings.
Each slice provides: 168 cal, 13 g pro, .5 g sat fat, 2 g unsat fat.

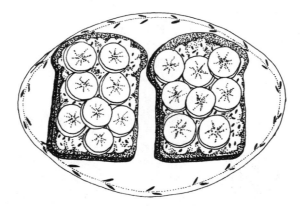

Skinny Kiwi Parfait

Enjoy the spirit of the ice-cream parlor at the breakfast table.

1 tablespoon peanut butter
1 tablespoon fruit juice
2 kiwis, cut in slices
2 tablespoons oat bran
    crunch, chopped nuts,
    or granola (see index for
    recipe)

½ cup low-fat yogurt or
    cottage cheese

Blend the peanut butter and fruit juice. Layer in a parfait glass the kiwi slices spread with peanut butter mixture and sprinkled with cereal or nuts. Top with yogurt or cottage cheese.
Yield: Makes 2 servings.
Each serving provides: 130 cal, 4 g pro, 1 g sat fat, 3.6 g unsat fat.

Reduced-Calorie Granola

This satisfying crunch is delicious with hot or cold milk or fruit juice. It is rich in fiber that aids digestion, lowers cholesterol levels, and aids in weight loss. The lecithin helps you to feel well fed on less food.

½ cup water
½ cup raisins
1 cup rolled oats
½ cup sunflower seeds
¼ cup sesame seeds
2 tablespoons unsweetened shredded coconut
¼ cup chopped almonds
½ cup wheat bran
2 cups popped corn
2 tablespoons lecithin granules
1 teaspoon cinnamon
1 tablespoon grated orange rind

Soak the raisins in the water for 2 hours or overnight.

In a large mixing bowl, combine the rest of the ingredients. Add the water in which the raisins were soaked. Mix with your hands or a wooden spoon to combine ingredients.

Preheat oven to 250°F. Spread the moistened mixture in a thin layer on a cookie sheet sprayed with non-fat baking spray, or lined with parchment paper. Place in oven and bake for 20 minutes or until the mixture is dry and crunchy. Stir in the raisins and bake 5 more minutes.

Microwave Method

Microcook water and raisins on high for 1 minute. Follow above instructions, but spread half of the moistened mixture in a microwave-safe dish about 12 by 9 inches and microcook, uncovered, on medium power for 5 minutes. Add the soaked raisins and microcook another minute. Stir it several times during the process. Leave it in the oven for about 5 minutes or until thoroughly dried out. Repeat the procedure with the other half of the mixture.

Yield: Makes about 2 quarts.

Each ½-cup serving provides: 72 cal, 2.5 g pro, 1 g sat fat, 5 g unsat fat.

Hot Apple Oat Bran Crunch

A delicious hot cereal to warm your innards on a blustery day.

¾ *cup oat bran crunch or other whole-grain cold cereal*
⅔ *cup apple juice*

1 *apple, chopped*
2 *tablespoons raisins or currants*
pinch of cinnamon

Combine the cereal, apple juice, chopped apple, raisins, and cinnamon in a 1-quart saucepan. Bring to a boil, lower heat, and simmer, stirring for 1 minute.

Microwave Method

Combine ingredients in a microwave-safe bowl and microcook on high for 30 seconds.

Yield: Makes 2 servings.

Each serving provides: 158 cal, 2.4 g pro, 1 g fat.

Slenderizing Fruit Cocktail

What a wonderful way to charge your batteries on a summer morning. Use cantaloupe, Casaba, Persian, or Crenshaw melon. For berries, use strawberries, raspberries, blackberries, loganberries, or blueberries.

> 2 melon slices or wedges
> 2 scoops of low-fat cottage
>   cheese (4 ounces each)

> ½ cup berries

Cut the melon in wedges. Top each with a scoop of cottage cheese. Garnish with berries.
Yield: Makes 2 romantic servings.
Each serving provides: 121 cal, 11 g pro, no fat.

Skinny Wheat Crepes

Treat yourself like royalty with this very-easy-to-assemble batter that never fails.

> 2 eggs plus 1 egg white (use
>   the extra yolk in the
>   filling)

> 1 cup water
> 1 cup whole wheat pastry
>   flour

In a large mixing bowl or food processor, combine eggs, flour, and water and mix to make a smooth batter the consistency of light cream. Pour into a 2-cup measure with a pouring lip and let stand for 1 hour. Heat an 8-inch nonstick skillet to medium high or until a little water dances when dropped into it. Pour ¼ cup of batter, thinly covering the entire surface, then tilt the pan and pour any excess batter back into the container. Cook until the top surface appears dry, and a peek underneath reveals that the bottom is golden, or until the top peels away from the pan. Bump the crepe out onto a tea towel. Fold the towel over it to prevent drying out. Repeat process.

Use as many crepes as you need. Freeze the rest. (See "Hot Tips for Great Crepes," page 64, for guidelines on freezing.)

For a complete breakfast, add 2 or 3 tablespoons of ricotta cheese as a filling. Just spoon into the center of each crepe and fold over both sides. Garnish with fresh fruit.

Yield: Makes about 16 crepes.

Each crepe provides: 35 cal, 2.8 g pro, .1 g sat fat, .2 g unsat fat.

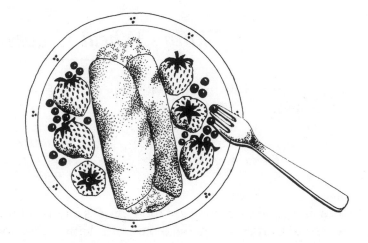

11
SMART BREAKFASTS FOR THE ALLERGIC

Wheat-Free Granola
Golden Kugel
Millet and Mushroom Pancakes
Mamaligge
Buckwheat Pancakes
Buckwheat Kasha Delight
Potato Starch Crepes
Rice Pudding

Some of the foods that are the most allergenic are those that are most frequently included in the breakfast menu; for instance: gluten, wheat, milk, eggs, citrus fruits, sugar, coffee, tea, corn, and chocolate. But don't despair. Even if you are among the 50 million people who suffer food allergies, you can wake up your life with a wide variety of delicious and nutritious morning meals.

SUBSTITUTIONS

In addition to the recipes presented in this chapter, you can follow any recipe in this book by making substitutions based on these guidelines:

Gluten Intolerance

Gluten is the protein in wheat that combines with yeast to make bread rise. Barley, oats, rye, and triticale also contain gluten but in lesser amounts than wheat. Hard wheat has more gluten than the soft wheat from which pastry flour is made. It is important to know that the most nutritious parts of the wheat, the wheat germ and the bran, have no gluten, and you can enjoy them in good health. Other grains that are gluten-free are corn, millet, rice, amaranth, and quinoa.

Wheat Intolerance

If you are allergic to wheat, you can use other grains like barley, rye, millet, rice, oats, amaranth, and buckwheat. Don't be confused by the name buckwheat. It is not related to wheat, not even a second cousin twice removed. Buckwheat is a member of the rhubarb family and is a very wholesome grain, rich in rutin, a bioflavonoid that strengthens cartilage.

Milk Intolerance

If you are allergic to milk, use herbal tea or fruit juice in recipes calling for milk. Or try these delicious nut milks:

Peanut Milk: Blend together ½ cup shelled, skinned peanuts with 2 cups of water. Strain. The chunks that remain can be added to granola or baked goods, or noshed on the spot.

Almond Milk: Blend together ½ cup almonds with 1 to 2 cups of water. Add small amounts of water at a time until achieving the desired consistency.

Sesame Milk: Blend ½ cup sesame seeds with ½ cup water, then add another cup of water, more or less depending on the consistency you prefer. Use less water when you want a substitute for cream.

Soy Milk: Combine 1 cup soy powder with 3 cups water in a large saucepan. Whisk until well dissolved. Bring to the boil over high heat, stirring constantly. Lower heat and simmer for 3 minutes. Serve hot or cold.

Many people who are lactose-intolerant can handle yogurt. While they lack lactase, the enzyme needed to digest the lactose in the milk, the fermentation process which converts milk to yogurt converts the lactose to lactic acid.

To make up for a lack of calcium, try these tips:

- Use blackstrap molasses as the sweetener in all baked goods, puddings, and confections. One tablespoon of blackstrap molasses provides 137 milligrams of calcium.
- Always use carob instead of chocolate. There is 4 times as much calcium in carob as there is in cocoa.
- An excellent source of calcium is sesame seeds—the brown ones with their hulls on. One hundred grams or slightly less than ¼ pound contains a whopping 1,160 milligrams of calcium. When they are hulled, they contain 100 milligrams of calcium.

- Look for tahini made from unhulled sesame seeds or make your own by grinding sesame seeds in a little seed mill or coffee grinder. Add a tiny bit of sesame oil to get peanut butter consistency.
- Add a little lemon juice to tahini—diluted with water—and it makes a great salad dressing.
- Combine tahini with ground coconut, sunflower seeds, and wheat germ. Add a bit of honey and blackstrap molasses and you have a dynamite confection—halvah.

Corn Intolerance

If you're allergic to corn and a recipe calls for cornstarch, substitute whole wheat flour, soy flour, brown rice flour, potato starch, or arrowroot starch. Most baking powders include cornstarch. Make your own corn-free baking powder by combining ¼ teaspoon bicarbonate of soda with ½ teaspoon cream of tartar. This is equivalent to 1 teaspoon baking powder. If you are on a strict salt-free diet, use potassium bicarbonate (available at most pharmacies) instead of sodium bicarbonate.

Egg Intolerance

If you're allergic to eggs, it may be just the white that is bothering you. In that case you can still enjoy the yolks.

Ducks' eggs can sometimes be handled by those allergic to hens' eggs.

Whether it's just the albumin or the whole egg you can't handle, remember that commercial egg substitutes are not egg-free. They contain egg whites and non-fat milk solids. (Also, make sure you're not given any vaccines produced in eggs. Vaccines for measles, mumps, rubella, and influenza are usually made with eggs.)

In baking, you can achieve the emulsifying effect of 1 egg by combining 2 tablespoons whole wheat flour, ½ teaspoon oil, ½ teaspoon egg-free baking powder (Royal Baking Powder contains no egg powder), and 2 tablespoons milk, water, or fruit juice. Or substitute 1 mashed banana, 1 tablespoon gelatin, or 1 tablespoon liquid lecithin for the missing egg. To thicken custard, substitute 1 tablespoon cornstarch for 1 egg.

Wheat-Free Granola

A good supply of wheat-free granola in the freezer is better than money in the bank. It is a complete protein cereal. Its wonderful flavors, crunch, and texture can be enjoyed by every member of the family, even those who can't handle wheat. The allergic child, then, does not feel different or deprived.

½ cup raisins
½ cup chopped prunes
1 cup hot water
3 cups uncooked rolled oats
    (not the instant)
½ cup unsweetened shredded
    coconut
½ cup unhulled sesame seeds
½ cup sunflower seeds

½ cup soy grits or flakes
¼ cup dry milk powder
    (optional)
1 teaspoon cinnamon
1 tablespoon grated orange
    rind (optional)
¼ cup oat bran
¼ cup rice bran (optional)
½ cup chopped cashews

Preheat the oven to 250°F.

Soak the raisins and prunes in the water for a few hours or overnight. Or place with liquid in a 1-quart bowl and microwave for 1 minute on full power.

In a large bowl, combine the oats, coconut, sesame and sunflower seeds, soy grits or flakes, milk powder, cinnamon, orange rind, oat bran, rice bran, and cashews.

Pour the water off the soaked fruit into a cup. Pour this liquid over the oat mixture and mix to moisten the grains. Spread this mixture on 2 cookie sheets lined with parchment paper, or greased with a mixture of a few drops of lecithin and oil, or sprayed with nonstick baking spray. Bake for 45 minutes, stirring every 15 minutes. Add the soaked raisins and prunes and bake for another 15 minutes. If the oats are not golden dry and crisp, bake for another 15 minutes. When the granola cools, store in tightly lidded containers. Keep refrigerated or frozen.

Microwave Method

Instead of placing the ingredients, mixed as described above, in the conventional oven, place parchment or wax paper on the bottom of the microwave. Spread about half the granola in a single layer and microwave on high for 2 minutes. Stir the ingredients and microwave for another 2 minutes. Add the raisins and microwave for 10 seconds. Repeat for the second batch. Store as above.

Yield: Makes 2 quarts.

Each ¼-cup portion provides: 76 cal, 3 g pro, 1 g sat fat, 2 g unsat fat.

Golden Kugel
(Wheat-, Gluten-, and Dairy-Free)

Have you ever enjoyed the rich, nutty flavor of millet, the tiny round yellow grains that resemble seeds? Millet is one of the most well-balanced and least allergenic of all the grains. It has the most complete protein and significantly more iron that other cereal grains. It is high in fiber, a good source of linoleic acid (an essential fatty acid so important for regulating cholesterol), and a richer source of minerals than any other cereal.

In this Kugel, the pleasing nutty flavor of millet is enhanced by the textural and flavorsome accents of apples, celery, and raisins.

3 cups water
1 cup millet grains
2 cups diced celery
2 cups grated apple
2 eggs, beaten

½ cup raisins
½ cup sunflower seeds
½ teaspoon cinnamon
1 teaspoon grated orange rind

In a large saucepan, bring the water to a boil. Add the millet gradually while stirring. Cook on low for 30 minutes or until all the water is absorbed. Blend the celery, apples, eggs, raisins, seeds, cinnamon, and orange rind into the cooked millet.

Preheat the oven to 350°F.

Spoon the mixture into a lightly oiled 9-inch-square baking dish and bake in oven for about 30 minutes. A real treat served hot with yogurt and blueberries, strawberries, or bananas.

Microwave Method (all procedures on high)

Combine water with 1 cup uncooked millet in a 2-quart casserole. Microwave, uncovered, for 18 minutes. Add the rest of the ingredients, cover with wax paper or 2 layers of paper toweling, and microwave for another 8 minutes.

Yield: Makes 8 servings. Leftovers can be refrigerated or frozen and reheated in a minute in the microwave.

Each serving provides: 148 cal, 6 g pro, 1 g sat fat, 3 g unsat fat.

Millet and Mushroom Pancakes
(Wheat-, Dairy-, and Gluten-Free)

When I make these for my wheat-allergic granddaughter, I make a lot because their appetizing aroma makes everyone hungry for them.

1 tablespoon olive or peanut oil
1 medium onion, diced
2 cups sliced mushrooms
2 tablespoons rice, soy, or garbanzo flour
1 tablespoon oat bran
¾ cup water
½ teaspoon vegetable seasoning or to taste
1½ cups cooked millet
⅓ cup sesame seeds for coating

In a small skillet, heat the oil and lightly sauté the onion and mushrooms.

In a saucepan, combine the flour and the oat bran. Add a tablespoon or two of water, just enough to make a smooth paste, then add the rest of the water and the seasoning. Bring the mixture to a boil, then reduce heat and simmer for about 2 minutes. Add the onion-mushroom mixture and simmer for a few minutes or until mixture is fairly thick. Add the cooked millet.

Preheat oven to 375°F.

Shape dough into about 10 round pancakes and coat with sesame seeds. Place them in a lightly oiled baking dish and bake for about 15 minutes. Or sauté them lightly in a heavy skillet.

Yield: Makes about 10 pancakes.

Each pancake provides: 74 cal, 4 g pro, 2 g unsat fat.

Mamaligge
(Wheat-, Dairy-, and Gluten-Free)

This is the dish that any Romanian would walk a mile for—in the rain. In Italy, they smother it with cheese and call it polenta. My kids call it cornmeal mush and love its rich nutty flavor.

4 cups water
1 cup cornmeal
1 teaspoon salt

In a large saucepan, bring the water to a boil, add the salt, then gradually add the cornmeal, stirring constantly. Lower the heat and continue to cook and stir until the mixture thickens— about 5 minutes. Continue to cook on low heat for about 15 minutes. Ladle into bowls and serve with applesauce for those who cannot handle dairy.

Offer yogurt, cottage cheese, melted cheese, or butter for those who can handle dairy.

Yield: Makes 5 servings.

Each serving provides: 115 cal, 2.6 g pro, .5 g fat.

Variation:

After the first 5 minutes of cooking, add ½ cup each of raisins and almonds. Continue cooking as above.

Microwave Method (all procedures on high)

To make mamaligge for 1 or 2, use:

> 4 *tablespoons cornmeal*
> 1 *cup water*
> ½ *teaspoon salt*

Combine all ingredients in a soup bowl or a 2-cup glass measure. Microwave for 1½ minutes. Stir, then cover loosely with wax paper or paper toweling, and microwave for another 1½ minutes.

Buckwheat Pancakes
(Wheat- and Gluten-Free)

As mentioned before, buckwheat's name should not fool those allergic to wheat: it is not a wheat, not even a close relative. Believe it or not, buckwheat is a respected member of the rhubarb family, and a valuable food for the allergic. It contains more high-quality protein than wheat, is high in fiber, is a good source of minerals, the vitamin

Bs, and rutin, a valuable anti-oxidant of the bioflavonoid family. It has fewer calories than wheat and is available dark or light. The light would probably be more acceptable to those who are not accustomed to buckwheat's robust flavor, but the dark has more fiber and a gutsy flavor that is relished by those who associate buckwheat with their culinary roots.

1 egg	1 tablespoon honey or molasses
1 cup skim milk	¾ cup sifted buckwheat flour
2 tablespoons olive oil or	¼ cup oat bran
melted butter	2 teaspoons baking powder

Preheat griddle over moderate heat while you are preparing the batter.

In mixing bowl or food processor, blend together the egg, milk, oil or butter, and honey.

In another bowl, combine the flour, oat bran, and baking powder. Combine the two mixtures and mix only until dry ingredients are dampened. Batter should be lumpy.

When a few drops of water on the griddle dance a jig, begin cooking the pancakes. Use about 3 tablespoons of batter for each. Do not crowd them. When bubbles form over the surface, turn gently and do the flip side. Turn one time only and try to turn them before the bubbles break. Stack them about 4 deep on heated plates and keep them warm in the oven while cooking the rest. Or, cook as many as you need and refrigerate the remaining batter for a quick breakfast on another day. Will keep in the refrigerator for 4 days and in the freezer for 3 months. Add another ½ teaspoon of baking powder before cooking the reserved batter. Serve with maple syrup, applesauce, sliced fresh fruit, or yogurt.

Yield: Makes about a dozen 4-inch pancakes.

Each pancake provides: 74 cal, 3 g pro, 1 g sat fat, 2 g unsat fat.

Buckwheat Kasha Delight
(Wheat-, Dairy-, and Egg-Free)

Buckwheat groats, from which the flour is derived, is better known as kasha, a word which triggers blips of nostalgia in the taste buds of everyone whose roots go back to Russia.

Kasha Delight is a breakfast dish that's festive enough to double as dessert.

2½ cups water	½ cup raisins
½ cup kasha	3 chopped dates (optional)
1 tablespoon honey	¼ cup shredded coconut

Bring the water to a boil and add the kasha, stirring. Add the honey, raisins, and chopped dates. Cook on medium-high heat for about 10 minutes. Stir in the coconut. Delicious served hot or cold.
Yield: Makes 4 servings.
Each serving provides: 228 cal, 1 g pro, 2 g fat.

Potato Crepes
(Wheat-Free)

These grain-free crepes are wonderful for those who can't handle gluten or grains and for Passover use. They are delicate and so thin you can see through them. Potato starch contributes lots of potassium—as much as 1,588 milligrams in 3½ ounces. It is also a good source of iron and calcium and provides vitamin C and some of the B vitamins, particularly niacin, which helps control cholesterol and, according to research from Hoffman-LaRoche, has qualities similar to those of some tranquilizers but without the side effects.

    3 eggs
    1 cup water
    ¾ cup potato starch

In mixing bowl or food processor, blend the eggs and water, then add the starch and blend to combine. Refrigerate for about 2 hours.

Heat a nonstick 6- or 7-inch skillet over medium-high heat until a drop of water bounces on it.

Pour about ¼ cup of batter onto the pan and tip it quickly so the batter spreads thinly over the entire surface. Return any excess to the batter bowl. Cook on 1 side only until the top begins to peel away from the pan. Bump it out, bottom side up onto a clean tea towel. Cover immediately with the other half of the tea towel. Repeat this procedure till the batter is used up. Be sure to stir the batter frequently and add more water as it thickens.

Yield: Makes about 16 crepes.

Each crepe provides: 39 cal, 2 g pro, 1.5 g fat.

Rice Pudding
(Wheat- and Gluten-Free)

There's something very comforting about rice pudding. Maybe that's because brown rice is a treasure trove of the B vitamins that put a nice warm glow on your disposition. Brown rice is a rich source of rice bran, which has been shown to effectively lower cholesterol levels. Rice is also the least likely of all the grains to cause an allergic reaction.

2 eggs	1½ cups cooked short-grain brown rice
2 cups milk	
¼ cup honey or rice syrup	½ cup raisins
1 teaspoon vanilla	dash of fresh grated nutmeg

Preheat oven to 350°F.

In a food processor or mixing bowl, blend together the eggs, milk, sweetener, and vanilla. Stir in the rice and raisins. Spoon into a 1-quart casserole and dust with nutmeg. Bake for 1 to 1½ hours. Pudding is done when a silver knife inserted in the center comes out clean. Serve hot with milk or cream or chill and serve plain or make it fancy with a whipped cream and fruit topping.

Microwave Method (all procedures on high)

Assemble all ingredients as above in a 1-quart, non-metal casserole. Place a deep, non-metal, 9-inch pie plate in the microwave oven. Place the filled casserole on the pie plate, then pour boiling water into the pie plate around the casserole about 1 inch deep.

Microwave, covered, for 4 minutes, then stir the mixture and continue to cook, still covered, for another 4 minutes or until the pudding is set around the edges and creamy in the center. Remove the casserole from the water and let it stand for about 10 minutes before serving.
Yield: Makes 6 to 8 servings.
Each of 6 servings provides: 192 cal, 8 g pro, 1.4 g fat.
Each of 8 servings provides: 144 cal, 6 g pro, 1 g fat.

Variation:
Omit 1 egg and add ¼ cup peanut butter.

12
SMART TOPPINGS
AND SPREADS

Healthy Heart Butter
Yogurt Creamless Cream Cheese
Sesame Tofu Spread
Fruit and Seed Spread
Crunchy Tofu Spread

Waffles, pancakes, muffins, and toast are frequently embellished with sauces, syrups, jams and jellies, sour cream, and gobs of butter, all of which can sabotage your slim-and-trim program and hasten the trip to Coronary Corners.

Don't get me wrong. I am very much in favor of embellishments that add moistness and flavor. But I want nothing to diminish the wholesomeness of the original recipe.

That's why I devised the following recipes to give you flavor and energizing nutrients at a very low cost in calories.

Healthy Heart Butter

This polyunsaturated butter banishes the fear of butter. It has an excellent country-fresh flavor and is rich in essential fatty acids. It has 4 times as much polyunsaturated fat as saturated. Since only 2 grams of polyunsaturated fat neutralizes the cholesterol-raising effect of 1 gram of saturated fat, this butter is a polyunsaturated wonder. The linseed oil that is blended with the butter is extremely rich in linolenic acid, which reduces the tendency of blood platelets to clump together and form clots in the arteries. Olive oil, which contributes 10 grams of monounsaturates, has been shown to reduce harmful cholesterol. But just because Healthy Heart Butter is better for you doesn't mean you should slather it on indiscriminately. All fats are high in calories and should be consumed in moderation.

*½ cup (1 stick) unsalted
    butter, cut in 8 pieces*
*¼ cup linseed oil (cold
    pressed), food quality*

*2 tablespoons safflower or
    sunflower oil*
1 tablespoon olive oil

Combine all ingredients in a blender or food processor and whiz for 2 minutes or until all ingredients are blended together. Mold into 2 small bowls and store in the freezer. May be used directly from the freezer. Use for spreading. For baking and sautéing, substitute olive or canola oil for the linseed oil.

Yield: Makes 1 cup.

1 tablespoon provides: 104 cal, 5.7 g sat fat, 22.7 g unsat fat.

Variation 1:
To further increase the cholesterol-lowering potential of Healthy Heart Butter, add 2 tablespoons of lecithin granules to the ingredients and

then process in the food processor or blender. Use this version for the table and for baking, or for sautéing.

Variation 2:
For Healthy Heart Butter to be used on pancakes, or waffles, or for baking muffins, add 1 to 2 tablespoons grated orange rind to the ingredients before processing.

Variation 3:
Instead of olive oil, use any of the following, which, according to *Controlling Cholesterol* (Bantam, 1988) by Kenneth H. Cooper, M.D., contribute the same amount of monounsaturates as 1 tablespoon of olive oil: 1½ tablespoons almond butter or 3½ tablespoons almonds; 2½ tablespoons peanut butter or ¼ cup peanuts; 3 tablespoons hazelnuts, 3½ tablespoons pecans, ¼ cup pistachios, 4 teaspoons canola oil (a new, unflavored mono oil made from rapeseed).

Variation 4:
To reduce the calories in Healthy Heart Butter, blend together 1 stick of butter, ¼ cup linseed oil, and ¼ cup yogurt or buttermilk. Use as a spread. *Only 84 calories in a tablespoon.*

Yogurt Creamless Cream Cheese

This tastes like cheese and spreads like cream cheese but it has ¼ the calories.

2 cups plain, low-fat yogurt   a drip bowl
  a colander lined with
    cheesecloth, or a clean
    tea towel

Place the colander lined with cheesecloth over the drip bowl. Pour the yogurt on top of the cheesecloth. Put the whole works in the refrigerator and let it drain for several hours or overnight. The drained liquid is whey, which is what Little Miss Muffet ate when she sat on a tuffet. The solids that collect in the colander are delicious cheese. You can store this in the refrigerator for up to two weeks. It is low in calories and rich in minerals. Use it in soups or in baking, or to make reduced-calorie cheese cakes.

Alternate Method for Draining
Line a coffeepot cone with filter paper. Place it over a coffeepot or other container that supports the cone without tipping. Ladle 1 pint of yogurt into the lined cone, place the whole works in the refrigerator to drain for 6 to 8 hours. The longer it drains, the firmer the cheese.
Yield: Makes 6 to 8 ounces depending on how firm you want it.
Each tablespoon provides: 20 cal, 1 g pro, .6 g fat.

Sesame Tofu Spread

This smooth, tasty spread is terrific on whole-grain toast, muffins, or bagels. It's high in energizing protein, very rich in calcium and the important fatty acids. Refrigerated, it will keep for about a week.

4 tablespoons soft tofu
2 tablespoons tahini (sesame butter)

1 tablespoon honey
1 teaspoon grated orange rind
pinch of cinnamon

Place all ingredients in a small bowl or food processor and process to blend ingredients.
Yield: Makes ½ cup or 8 tablespoons.
Each tablespoon provides: 30 cal, 1.4 g pro, 1.5 g unsat fat.

Fruit and Seed Spread

This is terrific as an alternate spread for jelly on toast or muffins.

1 medium-size Golden Delicious apple
1 tablespoon lemon juice
3 tablespoons soft tofu
1 teaspoon honey
½ cup toasted sunflower seeds

½ cup toasted sesame seeds
½ teaspoon cinnamon
1 tablespoon grated orange rind
pinch of nutmeg

Cut apple into thin slices and put it with the remaining ingredients in a blender or food processor. Whiz until ingredients are well blended and the mixture has a smooth consistency.

Yield: Makes 1 cup or 16 tablespoons.

Each tablespoon provides: 50 cal, 3.4 g pro, 2 g unsat fat.

Crunchy Tofu Spread

This high-protein, high-potassium, cholesterol-lowering bonanza is a pleasant combination of flavor and crunch.

½ cup oat bran crunch or ¼ cup oat bran	1 tablespoon maple syrup
	½ teaspoon vanilla
¼ cup soft tofu	½ teaspoon cinnamon
1 teaspoon lemon juice	1 teaspoon grated orange rind
½ banana, sliced	

Combine all ingredients in a blender or food processor and whiz until ingredients are well combined. It will not be perfectly smooth.

Yield: Makes about 1 cup.

Each tablespoon provides: 15 cal, 1 g pro, .4 g fat.

INDEX

Ask for these titles at your local bookstore or order today.

Use this coupon or write to: Newmarket Press, 18 East 48th Street, New York, N.Y. 10017 (212) 832-3575.

Please send me:

Jane Kinderlehrer's SMART BREAKFASTS: *101 Delicious, Healthy Ways to Start the Day*
_____$11.95, paperback, 192 pages (ISBN 1-55704-045-1)

Jane Kinderlehrer's SMART COOKIES: *80 Recipes for Heavenly, Healthful Snacking*
_____$9.95, paperback, 176 pages (ISBN 0-937858-62-5)

Jane Kinderlehrer's SMART MUFFINS: *83 Recipes for Heavenly, Healthful Eating*
_____$9.95, paperback, 176 pages (ISBN 0-937858-97-8)

Jane Kinderlehrer's THE SMART COOKIES/SMART MUFFINS GIFTSET
_____$19.90, paperback shrinkwrapped giftset, two volumes: 352 pages (176 pages each volume) (ISBN 1-55704-052-4)

For postage and handling, add $2.00 for the first book, plus $1.00 for each additional book. Please allow 4–6 weeks for delivery.

I enclose check or money order, payable to Newmarket Press, in the amount of $_____.

Name_____
Address_____
City/State/Zip_____

Clubs, firms, and other organizations may qualify for special discounts when ordering quantities of these titles. For more information, please call or write the Newmarket Special Sales Department at the above address.

                                    BOB 108901-KIND.KH